DESTINED TO LIVE
NINE LIVES

DESTINED TO LIVE NINE LIVES

A Kaleidoscope of

**Winning against Odds, a Life Story
of Lessons, Survival, and**

Turning Negatives into Positives!

PHYLLIS DUKE BA, MA

Library of Congress Control Number: 2010911263
ISBN: Hardcover   978-1-4535-4823-3
               Softcover   978-1-4535-4822-6
               Ebook   978-1-4535-4824-0

This book was printed in the United States of America.

To order additional copies of this book, contact:
Xlibris Corporation
1-888-795-4274
www.Xlibris.com
Orders@Xlibris.com
82581

CONTENTS

Dedication

To all the people who believed in me,
Who prayed for divine healing and God's intervention in my life,
To all the parents who have allowed me to educate
and train their children;
Teach them to pray to God; and show respect to their parents,
God, country, teachers, and leaders,
This book is only a humble tribute to God and
all His believers past and present
Who share in their travels in this life on earth
which often seems complex if not sometimes mysterious.

This effort is dedicated most of all to my children (Curtis Henry, Catherine Jones, and David Henry), who lived and learned as we endured happy and sad times together. Additional dedication is also being made to my late grandparents (Arthur and Gertrude Bauer, Edward and Ida Kellogg), who instilled in me a respect for joy, hardships, and our heritage; my late parents (Dorothy Bauer Kellogg and Wilbur Rhodes Kellogg), who always struggled to rise above their difficult circumstances; my late youngest sister, Nancy Jean Kellogg Christianson Pedersen, who retained her childlike, happy, and bubbly personality through indescribable physical suffering.

Furthermore, I want to honor my soul mates (Charline Altig Bonham, Deanna Franz Haynes, and Gloria Paulsen Duke), who each fought their own intense fights against cancer and chemotherapy until the very end; and even now, memories of their spirits, love of life, integrity, endurance, and vivaciousness in spite of cancer will live on forever. May God rest their souls and keep their spirits alive in our hearts and minds as we pray for strength and guidance to meet our own individual daily challenges which often seem small in comparison, but remembering the God who gave them peace and longsuffering will also guide our steps and meet our needs as He had promised to meet theirs.

PREFACE

It is my privilege and honor to know that God used the *Hour of Power* ministry to reach out, touch, and bring healing to the life of this young mother of three at the lowest point in her life. Fortunately, the *Hour of Power* was there when she was scanning the television one Sunday morning. She listened, found the address, and drove to the Crystal Cathedral. She tells me that the immediate love and acceptance she felt were overwhelming, and soon she became involved in a leadership role amongst the singles ministry at the cathedral. God has honored, blessed, and turned her scars into stars. She owns and oversees an ongoing and growing educational outreach program with a Christian emphasis for approximately five hundred children ages two through twelve for over thirty years in the greater Long Beach area.

Recognizing the parallels in her life coming from a farm in Iowa in 1956 in order for her young minister husband and their first baby to begin a ministry in California, but they soon met with emotional and marital tragedy after ministering in six different churches and ministerial positions. Thank God, however, that He reached down and restored her faith and reputation as she sought God's divine mercy, forgiveness, and guidance as a single mother of three working two jobs and attending college to further her education. We are pleased and thankful that she found respect and honor amongst our parishioners and was able to begin her life again.

Even though divorce is a tragedy which keeps on distributing its pain, she believed that the churches where people scorned and were critical of her were not appointed by God to be her judge and jury as they pretended to be. Our god is a loving and forgiving god who alone knows and understands the reasons why certain tragedies are allowed to happen in this life. Tapestry which looks so confusing and disorganized from our human analytical perspective is truly beautiful when God is the ultimate designer orchestrating and guiding our lives from heaven above.

May God continue to bless this shining light as she touches lives for His honor and glory every day of her life.

Dr. Robert H. Schuller
Senior pastor, Crystal Cathedral 1955-2009
Garden Grove, California

Phyllis @
age 3

CHAPTER 1

ABORTION ABORTED

The Depression years had set in, and families were under great financial and emotional stress. My parents, Wilbur Rhodes Kellogg and Dorothy Margaret Bauer, were joined in marriage on July 3, 1931. You might say that their marriage began with a big bang. Shortly after the wedding ceremony, Wilbur walked over to join Dorothy, who was sitting on the sofa. No sooner had he put his arms around her and begun to give her a kiss than fireworks began shooting off in his back pocket. He had been planning to have fireworks ready for their Fourth of July celebration the next day. Little could anyone imagine that on the same evening of their wedding, he would be seeking emergency medical attention at the local hospital in St. Paul, Minnesota!

Wilbur had been working at Montgomery Ward department store in the tire division in South St. Paul, Minnesota, where he was soon to be laid off due to the Depression along with hundreds of other workers, most of whom also had families to support. His wages were meager and barely enough to pay for rent, food, gas, and any other necessary expenses.

Dorothy had been teaching in a rural school, grades kindergarten through eighth grade, with a respectable salary. Life looked rosy enough; however, only three weeks into the marriage, Dorothy became violently ill with frequent nausea and vomiting. Obviously, she had become pregnant, and this pregnancy was not agreeing with her at all. With the exception of a severe illness shortly after her own birth when she was only five weeks old, she had been considered healthy during her twenty-one years. Born in 1910 before the age of antibiotics, she had not been expected to live. Quoting from a letter written in January of 1911, her uncle said, "Art Bauer's baby has been continually having convulsions, the doctors have done everything they could and now their baby is not expected to live through the night." Whether there was an underlying physical condition which caused Dorothy to become violently ill during pregnancy would never be known.

Family members became alarmed for the newly married couple, and Dorothy always believed that relatives were of the opinion that she should not be having a baby at this time, first of all, due to the Depression and secondly due to the severity of her pregnancy-related sickness. After taking into account the concerns of family members, she firmly aborted the idea of having an abortion as an option and set out to endure the remaining eight and a half months of vomiting, dizziness, and an excruciatingly painful childbirth. Clearly, this author would not have lived to tell this story of such an eventful and rewarding life had there been an abortion. Christians were not allowed to consider abortion unless a mother's life was in imminent danger. Abortion was considered to be murder during that era and would have been considered a serious tragedy. Certainly, the last thing Dorothy and Wilbur wanted was to have the stigma of having had an abortion or such a tragedy in their lives. It makes one wonder about the thousands and thousands of abortions performed each year. How many of those babies would have miraculous stories to tell today had they been given the opportunity to live? A great amount of ridicule was cast toward Wilbur and Dorothy over the years for their genuine respect for life and their belief in God. Warning comments were frequently offered regarding raising their children in a Christian home. The concern was that children raised in such a strict Christian home would surely turn against religion, society, and their own parents when they grew up.

It is also interesting that Dorothy had become a Christian by accepting Jesus as her personal savior when she was a young teenager. Even though her family was basically Christian in name, very little spiritual life seemed to be evident in their daily lives. Wilbur also made a decision to become a Christian during his courtship period with Dorothy. Wilbur had first met Dorothy briefly when she was thirteen. He had accompanied his older brother Ernest from their home in River Falls, Wisconsin, in order to seek work on the Bauer Dairy Farm near Mason City, Iowa. That mere acquaintance left a lasting impression, which would kindle for five years until he was able to make the long trip back to Mason City and seek her hand in marriage. She had turned eighteen and was beginning to date and certainly was not interested in Wilbur's sudden interest and proposal for marriage. He said that he had waited five years to go and ask her to marry him. He never dated anyone else but simply waited for the girl of his dreams. This was quite a shock to Dorothy, who seemed somewhat put off at his apparent sudden and intense interest in her. She knew, for one thing, that since she was a new Christian, she would never marry someone who wasn't a Christian. This began a standoff from the start; however, three years later, Wilbur also sought spiritual guidance and placed his faith in Jesus as his personal savior. Now that Dorothy had completed her college work for her teaching credential and had begun teaching in the little town of Fertile, Iowa, she was content to stay single and continue dating. Wilbur, however, came back again and again with his proposal for marriage. He said that he had known that she was the one for him when he met her when she was only thirteen. He indicated that he would never give up pursuing her until she would finally say yes. His newfound faith, constant prayers for her protection, and their potential future together with him finally made the difference in her attitude; and she finally accepted his proposal for marriage. The wedding date was set for July 3, 1931.

My mother's pregnancy with me was extremely difficult. Nine months seemed like an eternity to her. Not only had Wilbur been laid off due to the Depression, but times were also already very difficult. Friends who would last a lifetime rallied to comfort and support both Dorothy and Wilbur. Living near the St. Paul Bible Institute was a blessing. Not only could a few students room and board with Dorothy and Wilbur, generating rent and providing a meager income, but Dorothy was also able to attend some classes at the St Paul Bible Institute for her own personal edification and for further educational advancement. "Friends helping friends" became their lifetime motto.

Right on schedule, exactly ten months after their marriage, on May 3, 1932, I entered the world. Known as little Phyllis Louise, I was born, weighing in at seven pounds and six ounces. I would be surprisingly healthy from the start, especially after such a turbulent pregnancy and childbirth. Soon I became the center of attention, especially from my father. "She's worth more than a million dollars," he used to say. Hearing that comment at a very young age seemed to help me place a very high value on my life. Of course, that idea also helped to form a good self-image, which would become critically important later in life.

Early years as a baby were spent with family and friends. My mother regained normal health and happiness. My father continued searching for ways to make a comfortable living for his little family. Since he had many talents as well as a bubbly personality and was also extremely handsome, he was able to find work everywhere he looked; and in spite of the Depression, he was able to make life comfortable for his family. He also knew that money was not the most important thing in life. Family, friends, faith, attending church, fishing, deer hunting, raising cocker spaniel puppies, helping others, having fun, and enjoying life were all important to him during those years of hardship and struggle.

Early achievements in my life included learning to tie my shoes at three years of age. Hours of trying again and again until finally succeeding required great self-determination. This early persistence and self-determination would reinforce my efforts for many gigantic challenges which were to lie ahead in my life. Additionally, the ability to make the right choices and realize the consequences of one's actions was also necessary for me to begin to learn at age three. I have vivid recollections at that young age of a neighbor boy, also three, who encouraged me to help pick all the tomatoes from a neighbor's garden and throw them down over a steep bank onto the street below. This little episode of having fun throwing tomatoes as far as we could was met with shockingly strict discipline at home and a new awakening of the meaning of being able to think and make the right choice as well as to learn how to respect other people's property.

Another recollection had to do with recognizing emotions. I distinctly sensed jealousy on the part of my mother as I overheard conversations which caused me to wonder why my mother seemed upset by my father's constant attention to me. Later when I was five, I had climbed onto the couch to snuggle next to my father. Again I sensed a depth of jealousy from my mother as she abruptly scolded me and told me to get down and never to lie close to my father again because that was something that little girls don't do. I began to surmise a deep jealousy which would rear its head again and again throughout my lifetime. This outburst on the part of mother caused my father to withdraw from me emotionally; and therefore, he never, ever, showed any physical display of affection toward any of his three daughters again during his whole lifetime. That meant never a kiss, hug, or even a pat on the back. On the contrary, he would always demonstrate affection, respect, and appreciation toward my girlfriends. He showed his appreciation toward them by incessantly teasing them. The absence of his demonstration of any affection toward me contrasted with the constant attention to my girlfriends caused me to become inwardly upset and angry at times. Years later, I began to understand the underlying reason for the seemingly cool "businesslike" relationship which he showed toward me. Interestingly enough, many years later when grandchildren finally arrived, all bets were off. He would then become warm, cordial, loving, and very expressive in his feelings for them. I believed that the generational distance gave him permission to express his loving and caring emotions which had been pent up for all those years. Additionally, the grandchildren were perhaps not a threat to his marriage as perhaps my mother thought that his eldest daughter might become.

CHAPTER 2

DEPRESSION YEARS

The Depression years became the glue that cemented many families and friends together. It was an understatement that times were hard and difficult. Many people turned to drinking alcohol to ease or erase their problems. One couple that we knew divorced, which at that time was almost unheard of in the Midwest. Marriage was considered a contract for life, and if couples had difficulty getting along, they seemed to grin and bear it or at least keep their troubles to themselves while they continued in their marriage until death.

People began to draw upon their own ingenuity and creativity in ways that might not have surfaced in normal times. My uncle Ed Kellogg began inventing tools. He accumulated hundreds of patents. Uncle Earnest Kellogg began farming in River Falls, Wisconsin. Uncle Oliver Kellogg began a newspaper business in Warroad, Minnesota. Aunt Katherine Kellogg finished college and began teaching school. My parents moved to Mason City, Iowa and took over ownership of the former Bauer Family Dairy. Uncle Lynn Bauer began building radios to sell; and his younger brother, my uncle Kenneth, assisted on the Bauer farm and trained horses for the rodeo and the county fair. He also took up boxing and entered in several matches on Saturday nights in Mason City.

My mother suddenly became severely ill again, much like in her first pregnancy. Yes, she was expecting again; and this time her symptoms were even more serious, if that were possible. Soon an African American maid arrived and began cooking meals, doing the laundry, and caring for us. Mother was confined to her bed for the remaining eight and a half months. Meanwhile, a new baby sister, Margaret Ann, and nicknamed Peggy, was born on August 22, 1936. That birth experience was so severe that she was termed a blue baby who was not expected to live. She did, however, revive and return to normal color after several hours. The doctor recommended a full hysterectomy as soon as possible for my mother, and she was told that she should never have another child.

My father worked hard building up the Kellogg Dairy Business. Activities concerning the dairy became my earliest recollections of business. Evenings were spent sorting coins and rolling them into packets to be taken to the bank. Unknowingly, this experience probably left an indelible imprint in my brain as I have since always realized the importance of each and every penny and the fact that it takes a lot of organization and teamwork to make a business run smoothly and successfully. Tales over the dinner table regarding the customers on the dairy route and their personal experiences were often discussed. One of the most exciting stories was the morning when my father delivered milk at 4:30 a.m. to the Brendel home and was greeted at the door. "Come on in and see our new twin baby girls who were born during the night," said Mr. Brendel. Obviously, I thought that having twins must have been the most exciting happening in the whole world. It turned out that years later I would personally know those twins and would attend school with their older brother, Don.

My father was soon able to purchase a new 1937 Plymouth panel delivery truck for the dairy. What a proud day that was when he drove up with his sparkling white panel truck. Everything seemed to be going well with the dairy business. The Kellogg Dairy became very popular in its six years of duration, and we were proud as a family to have been able to purchase a new house located at 203 Crescent Drive in Mason City during that time. Well, everything seemed to be going smoothly until I sensed some very strained and unusual conversations going on in our home. Something seemed to be going wrong with the dairy business. There was a lot of hush-hush talk which no one ever figured out for sure except to know that an argument had occurred between Grandmother Bauer and Dorothy's youngest brother, Kenneth, regarding ownership of the dairy business, which evidently was somehow secured by the mortgage on our new home on Crescent Drive. The mystery regarding the abrupt closing of the Kellogg Dairy remains unknown to this very day. Ultimately and unfortunately, this meant moving out of our lovely little home on Crescent Drive. We temporarily moved our family into my grandmother Bauer's family farm homestead until arrangements could be made to rent the Colonel MacNider farm, which was vacant while he was overseas serving in the armed forces during World War II.

Peggy was an adorable baby who stole the hearts of everyone who saw her. Her hair changed from black to a beautiful light blond, and with her blue eyes, she was picture-perfect. No sooner was she attempting to crawl than I contracted an infection from nonpasteurized milk. Bacteria spread to my heart, and soon I developed rheumatic fever. I was just five years old. This meant that I was to be kept quiet, in bed and at home, until the infection could heal. A sulfa drug, which was the only known medication for infections, was administered twice a day. I had to withdraw from kindergarten, which I really missed. Since I was quick to make friends and join in activities, I was really saddened by being bedridden for nearly nine months. It took a lot of understanding to overcome the urge to get out of bed and play, but knowing and understanding the consequences caused me to cooperate. Eventually, I would learn that this would pay off with a clean slate of perfect health.

My mother became involved with my care during my illness with rheumatic fever, and consequently, she delayed the hysterectomy which her doctor had required after the birth of her second baby. Yes, once again she was struck down with violent illness due to a third pregnancy. This time she was required to stay completely flat and in bed for the entire nine months, and once again, we had another African American maid, Mrs. Washington. She frightened me by telling me that when I grew up, I might need to have my toes cut off because I was putting too much white sugar on my cereal. Unfortunately, my love for sugar outweighed my fear of having my toes cut off; however, I often remembered her comments throughout my life. Evidently, Mrs. Washington, who was quite overweight, might have had diabetes herself or had a family member who had to have an amputation due to diabetes; nevertheless, she tried and tried to persuade me to stop using sugar. She was unsuccessful in weaning me from white sugar.

Nancy was born in yet another very traumatic childbirth on September 5, 1938. She was a beautiful baby, and somehow, due to my mother's weakened physical condition, baby Nancy was placed in a home with Mr. and Mrs. Hollister for approximately a year. I recall going to visit her at least once during that time and years later found a picture of myself at about age seven, looking at Nancy in her baby buggy with Mrs. Hollister. Nancy was the most beautiful of all babies. She was happy, had beautiful curly light brown hair, looked like Shirley Temple, and always won the hearts of everyone. Nancy never recalled the time in her life when she was cared for by another couple until I spoke about it with her late in her life and in the last few months before she passed away with an undiagnosed lung disease. I also remember that at about age eighteen months Nancy fell out of her high chair onto her head, after which she began stuttering. She often had to try very hard to overcome her tendency to stutter, but conquer it she eventually did. She retained her bubbly, lovable personality throughout her entire life. She also was a very caring and giving person who often exceeded her means in order to purchase gifts for friends and family even though she really could not afford to shower others with gifts; therefore, she relied on credit cards to support her giving.

When we were very young, people would often comment, "Peggy is just beautiful and Nancy is very cute, but Phyllis is just precious!" That really didn't make sense to me. Peggy, as we had nicknamed her, was jovial and fun loving. She and Nancy spent endless hours playing with their only doll, Jimmy. They also cut out paper dolls and played "pretend" for endless hours. They made the dining-room table into their house, and Jimmy became their child. Later on the farm when playing outside, Nancy would sit on her haunches (partially in the air, but not on the ground) and pick kernels of corn off from an ear of dried corn, dropping them one at a time on the ground to feed our chickens. The chickens usually waited patiently for each kernel to drop as they cackled and crowed with delight. Occasionally a ruckus would erupt, and often, a full-fledged fight amongst the chickens might ensue. Startled as she would be, she would never stop picking off the kernels until the empty corncob was ready to be thrown away.

Peggy really liked our neighboring farmer's little boy, Jimmy Douglas. She was about four when she was sitting on our Shetland pony in the front yard. We had been taking turns riding the pony, and we were all watching Peggy when it was her turn. Suddenly, there was a loud clap of thunder in the distance upon which the pony jolted forward and began running as fast as he possibly could. He ran out our long driveway, out onto the busy highway, and galloped over a half a mile to Jimmy Douglas's house. Peggy miraculously held on tight for the fastest ride of her life. Frantically, my parents jumped into the car and brought her back home safe and sound. We were all very thankful that she did not fall off or was struck by a car on the highway. Another day after Peggy had been playing with Jimmy Douglas, she came into the house and jumped on the bed where our parents were resting and shrieked at the top of her lungs, saying, "Jimmy Douglas and I are going to get married! We just decided today!" This, of course, became a funny joke which my mother told many times.

Nancy, being the youngest of three sisters, had a personality that was winsome and bubbly. She retained this same "childlike" bubbly personality throughout her lifetime. We didn't have any of the usual toys that other children seemed to have, but our parents raised cocker spaniel puppies to sell. The puppies as well as other baby animals on the farm provided many hours of loving enjoyment.

There was four and a half and six and a half years' difference in ages between my sisters and myself. This translated into a large age difference where each of us had different interests and experiences as we grew up. Peggy was thirteen and Nancy eleven when I left for college. My few visits back to my parents' home were mostly after they were in their late teens and they were out and about with their friends at those times, so our paths rarely crossed. We never corresponded and rarely communicated with each other until nearly fifty years later when our mother needed full-time care. During the time when I was 100 percent responsible for my mother's care, I began making phone calls to my sisters, inquiring if either of them could take Mother into their home for a while. Each of them said they would be unable to do that, and therefore, I was left with total responsibility for my mother for twenty-seven years, which included handling her finances, medical appointments, and treatments; caring for her home and automobile; and eventually providing full-time care in my home. I called each one, Peggy and Nancy, frequently during this time in order to discuss the many complications which I encountered in caring for our mother. Those conversations opened the door for renewing our family ties and comparing memories from our early childhood years. It was during some of those conversations that I learned that neither sister remembered much if anything about me when as children we lived at home. They felt that they had grown up as two very close sisters in a totally different family setting than I had. I never remember playing with them, except for being their babysitter, and caring for them on several occasions when they were too young to remember. When I was required to be kept in bed for several months during my illness with rheumatic fever, they were playing together in a different portion of our home. They were probably kept away from me in an effort to keep me quiet as the doctor had ordered. Being older, and after my extended illness, I was allowed to visit my friends and their families in their homes for weekends and summer camps. I was taught to ice-skate and ski very early, and neither sister was ever involved in any sports. I had a self-imposed determination to enter college on the very Monday morning after I graduated from high school and then to work and support myself throughout college so I could secure an advantage in my future career. Neither of my sisters showed aspirations for college degrees even though my parents financed one term for each of them in college. There seemed to be a large divergence between us regarding our interests, and this remained true for most of our lives. It took some effort to overcome this chasm during the period when my mother was 85 percent paralyzed and I was caring for her in my home. There were times when I was brought to tears over the almost impossible dilemma of how to physically and emotionally care for our mother. Even though I eventually hired nurse assistants on a twenty-four-hour basis, the stress, emotional, and physical strain were almost beyond human capabilities.

As the older sister and the babysitter for the two younger siblings when I was merely seven or eight, I knew how to feed them, change diapers, and do everything that caring for little children would require. It never occurred to me that I was too young to have full charge of my two younger sisters for hours at a time during the day, evening, or into late-night hours. Perhaps my parents were out seeking ways to make a better living, purchasing groceries, or visiting with friends. I never knew where they were. I only recall two episodes when I knew that I was not up to the task. The first one was when we heard loud rattling at the windows and the doors. Someone was definitely trying to get in, or so we thought. I took both of them with me to hide in the back of a closet of a second-floor bedroom where we remained silent and completely motionless for perhaps two or three hours. Our parents finally returned home to find everything all right except for three badly frightened children. At that time, we were staying in our grandmother's home in the country at least five miles from town and a quarter of a mile from the nearest neighbor. It crossed my mind at that time that one of our neighbors might even have been the person trying to enter our house or at the least trying to scare us since our neighbors might have been aware that our parents were not at home.

After all, one of our neighbors had threatened and forced me against the wall of his barn when I was sent to return an empty milk can and to purchase more milk at that farm. I was in shock as the neighbor grabbed me, thrusting himself against me, and forcing me tightly up against the wall. He gestured toward his gun, which he said was loaded and which he told me he would use if I ever told anyone about what he was going to do to me. Already, I was frightened to ever be alone in the presence of any of my neighbors. I have been thankful that in my struggle to free myself and upon saying a silent prayer, I immediately felt unusual strength surging within which allowed me to wiggle and slither from his clutches. Many years later, I confronted this neighbor regarding his criminal actions and intentions, stating that I felt that my innocence was ruined when I was merely twelve years old. He said that he really hadn't hurt me very much and that I should just forget about it. Of course, this happened to me many years before I was aware of any laws protecting women and children. I would have never thought of calling the police but would have expected retaliation if I were to tell anyone about this attempted rape. Experiences like this one, which was only the first of many in my life, make it easy for me to understand the plight of rape victims. I challenge young girls to use caution at every turn in their life and utilize spiritual guidance, inward determination, strength, and skill to win against a stronger sex-driven child predator. Other women who shared similar experiences from this person began whispering about their traumatic encounters with this person; however, not one of us broke ranks and told authorities. It was understood that things of a sexual nature were to be kept "hush-hush."

Another frightening experience happened one night when a light bulb burned out in the bathroom. I knew where there was a new bulb; and just as I inserted it into the socket, it exploded like a fire bolt, shattering thin pieces of glass everywhere while leaving us in total darkness. God only knows how we survived such traumatic experiences without adults around to comfort or guide us, but survive we did and the lessons we learned seemed to make us stronger.

One of the creative things my mother did in order to earn money during the Depression was to become a salesperson for *Highlights for Children* magazine, the *World Book Encyclopedia*, and even for a food supplement called Nutrilite. Mother would go alone or sometimes gather us into the car, drive to town, stop in a residential area, and tell us to wait in the car while she went door-to-door to sell those products. She had a delightful, bubbly, and persuasive personality and could convince almost anyone to buy something from her. She really believed in the products which she was selling, and that made her message much more persuasive. Several hours later, she would return with $20 or more. That would mean that we could go to the grocery store and buy food for the next few days. She also was very resourceful in planting a garden, canning fruits and vegetables, and even growing bean sprouts under the kitchen sink to supplement our meager meals with extra protein. My father also raised calves, pigs, chickens and ducks for meat and eggs. I learned how to kill a rooster with an ax when I was no more than ten years old. That may have seemed difficult; however, the hardest job of all was plucking out the feathers, singeing the remaining down and tiny pinfeathers, and then cleaning out the inside of the chicken.

New clothing was almost unheard of during those years of hard times at least in our family. Two of my cousins in their late twenties and/or early thirties were fortunate enough to have government jobs, and they were able to shop and wear stylish clothing. Ethel Ridgeway was the Cero Gordo County treasurer, and Joy Johnson was the Cero Gordo County clerk. They were able to afford nice clothing and willingly donated their used clothing to my family. My mother was an innovative and clever seamstress, and she redesigned and refitted many nice-looking outfits for the three of us girls. The outfits retained an older-adult look; however, I was thankful to have nice, warm clothing, especially in the winter months. I was sixteen years old before I remember a new dress or suit being purchased for me. It was a red suit, very plain in appearance, but I could be seen wearing that same red suit to almost every event. Jeans had not been invented as yet, so as a young girl I alternated between cotton or corduroy slacks or the made-over dresses, as I called them. Women wore dresses; they never wore pants, which were called slacks, even when ice-skating, riding horseback, or skiing. Girls were never allowed to wear slacks with a zipper down the front, as those pants were considered to be boys' clothing only. Additionally, girls in our church circle were never allowed to wear any makeup or earrings. We were told that it would be better to look like we were painted by angels than by the devil himself.

Some of the places where we lived did not have indoor bathrooms, and during those times, we arranged to visit our cousin Ethel Ridgeway on a weekly basis for family baths. That would mean a big family trip to town late in the evening with our nightclothes packed. After we each took turns in the old fashioned bathtub which had feet that looked like a tiger's feet and was filled to the brim with very warm water and bubbles six inches thick, we would dress in our pajamas and be ready for bed by the time we drove fifteen to twenty minutes to our home again.

During the third grade, our family had met the crises regarding the dispute over the Kellogg Dairy Business, which required that we move temporarily into our grandmother's home out in the country. This meant that I had to transfer from Wilson Elementary School, leaving my many friends and enrolling in Jefferson Elementary School, where I didn't know anyone. Within a short time, I took up playing the violin, joined Girl Scouts, and became the best gymnast on the parallel bars in the whole school. Since we lived five miles out of town, I either had to be driven to school, ride my bicycle, or carpool with some cousins of mine who also lived on farms. My popularity was tested during the fifth grade when I became ill and again missing several months of school with a recurrence of rheumatic fever.

During this time, which was prior to air transportation, a man with a large red wooden cargo-type airplane came to our city. He advertised rides for $25 each, and my father purchased two tickets and took me for the airplane ride. The plane had benches around on the inside but no individual seats or seat belts. We had about a half-hour flight in which the plane only got about one hundred feet above the trees. It seemed as if the plane was struggling to stay in the air, but we landed safely and I became one of a very few people who had flown in an airplane in the mid-1930s. The next flight that plane took was in another city, but it never could make it above the trees and it crashed soon after it took off. That did not, however, discourage me from flying in small planes. Three of my cousins and one of my uncles became licensed pilots, and my father also took all the required flying lessons in order to earn his pilot's license. He always became airsick when he had to perform loops and fly upside down. This kept him from being able to receive his pilot's license, and he probably never could have enjoyed owning his own airplane and flying as much as he wanted. He was anxious for me to learn to fly also. That is something I planned to do, but I never did reach that goal.

During the Depression, families really seemed to care about other people and helped each other in times of need. As soon as we were old enough, which meant ten years old or thereabouts, we were expected to be in the fields pulling weeds, driving the tractor, cultivating the corn, harvesting the wheat or beans, loading bales of hay, or doing whatever jobs needed to be done. It didn't matter if you were a girl or a boy; if you lived on a farm, you would also be expected to work. Some of the younger children helped prepare meals and delivered the food to the workers in the fields. Families took turns concentrating all their efforts and family members to work on one farm at a time. That meant that everyone would arrive at 6:00 a.m. at the designated farm and no one would leave until long after dark or at least until that job was finished on that particular farm, and then everyone and all the workers would move with all the farm equipment and themselves in a big caravan to the next farm.

Pulling weeds in the fields was an all-day job. The pay was 1¢ for every ten weeds and then only if the full root was pulled out rather than broken off. It was possible to work very hard and long for all day and possibly not even earn a dollar.

CHAPTER 3

WORLD WAR II

W alking through the kitchen on December 7, 1941, while we were temporarily living at my grandmother's house, I noticed that the radio near the kitchen sink was turned on; and I heard the announcer on the radio say, "We are at war. The Japanese have just bombed Pearl Harbor in Hawaii." What an emotionally shocking thought. The teakettle on the wood-burning kitchen stove was steaming, ready for tea or coffee. Grandmother had a fresh batch of oatmeal cookies cooling on the shelf above the stove. How I loved her oatmeal cookies, which were full of raisins and walnuts. I was just nine years old and had just been thinking about practicing my gymnastic routine for school and getting ready to attend the basketball game on Friday night. Until now, I had heard only a few discussions regarding World War I, but the thought of war was far from my mind. There were twelve of us girls nearly the same age who attended the Christian and Missionary Alliance church on Delaware Avenue in Mason City. Our pastor, Rev. Lowell Young, was a leader who motivated us to become the best Christians we could possibly be. His sermons kept us focused on scripture verses in the Bible and how they applied to our lives. He and his many guest evangelists encouraged us to think about becoming a missionary someday when we grew older. We were very concerned about people in other countries who had never heard about God or the Bible. He said that millions of people around the world had never heard of God or His Son, Jesus. I had very limited knowledge of the multitudes of people around the world. Neither he nor anyone else that I knew ever mentioned to us that war could happen at a moment's notice, so I felt that we were truly caught off guard. Nevertheless, I continued walking through the kitchen but at a faster pace, as I wanted to tell my father and the workers who were taking a break from feeding and milking the cows in the barn. Everyone stopped and listened in disbelief as I told them about the bombing of Pearl Harbor and that our country was at war.

Life became more intense. Riding my pony was not as much fun. School seemed more serious, and we began having air-raid drills every day at school. Every student was required to walk silently in a single file to the basement of our school building, pass the coal furnace, and the boiler room, where we would stand quietly for bomb-raid drills. Making a popping sound with my tongue during one of the drills became an offense which my teacher noticed immediately. We literally had to be totally quiet.

It was the same year, 1941, when I was in fifth grade, that I had suffered a remission of rheumatic fever. This time, the doctor became concerned about permanent damage which might leave me with a heart murmur. I was confined to bed for six months. My tenth birthday was on May 3, 1942, and the whole fifth-grade class took a field trip by bus and came four miles out of town to my home for a picnic. We lived at that time in a rented house on a lovely acreage that we named the Hoffler Place, after Mrs. Hoffler, who had lived there for many years. It was about four miles cast of Mason City and directly across from the MacNider farm, where we had lived previously for a year. All during this time I was attending Jefferson Elementary School. I had previously ridden my bicycle those four miles to and from school many times when the weather was nice. I kept my pony in the front yard until he had to be sold. My classmates all lived in the city. They were very excited to visit me in the country, and I was equally happy for their company. Mrs. Hartman was our teacher.

Later in June when it was time for report cards to be issued, Mrs. Hartman wrote that she would require me to repeat the fifth grade since I had missed so much school. She had refused to send books to my home during that whole year. Now Mrs. Hartman was Catholic and had made it known that she didn't like Protestants, and I wondered if this was why she was withholding her cooperation regarding providing homework for me. This was a time when my mother really went to bat for me. She had a conference with Mrs. Hartman in our classroom on the second floor of the school, but Mrs. Hartman was quite angry and continually insisted that I would need to repeat the fifth grade. Then mother walked up the steps to the third floor to our principal's office and talked to Ms. Nicholas, our school principal. Ms. Nicholas was quite disturbed that Mrs. Hartman had refused to send homework for me to keep up on my lessons at home. She never wanted Mrs. Hartman to know that she interceded on my behalf, but Ms. Nicholas told my mother to walk to the lawn in front of the school, directly below her office, and she would secretly throw the schoolbooks which I would need out from the third-floor window to the ground for my mother to pick up. She did not want Mrs. Hartman to see my mother carrying the books through the hallway. My mother had previously been a public-school teacher, and she tutored me for the next several weeks until I completed all the required work. Ms. Nicholas, the principal, then signed my report card and promoted me to the sixth grade. This surprised and again angered Mrs. Hartman. When I returned to school in the fall as a sixth grader, she never mentioned my promotion or ever spoke to me again.

It had been during the previous summer of 1941 when we were invited to visit our former pastor, Rev. Paul Freleigh, and his family, who were on leave from the mission field in Brazil. They were living temporarily in New York City on Manhattan Island during their furlough. Nothing ever seemed to stop my parents from taking advantage of an opportunity. The next thing I knew, we were packed and driving in our 1939 De Soto on our way to visit the Freleigh family in New York and then to the World's Fair in New York City. Somehow, the decision was made to leave my two younger sisters, Peggy, nearly five, and Nancy, who would be three in September, with friends during our two-week trip to New York City.

Riding in the backseat while we were driving those many miles seemed to be one big driving lesson for me. I sat or stood in the backseat and almost never took my eyes off the road except for the time when I sat down and unknowingly sat on a bumblebee that had flown in the window. I have only had two bee stings in my life. That first time was almost as traumatic as the next time. When I was thirteen, I was hanging clothes in the backyard at our home when a thunderstorm was approaching. I was reaching up to take down clothes from the clothesline when I saw a flash of light streak across the sky, striking a large airplane. The plane burst into flames within seconds, and I watched in shock as the plane with smoke curling from it went into a tailspin heading straight toward our neighbor's farm. I ran quickly to climb onto the chicken house to see where the plane was landing. I disturbed a hornet's nest in my haste, and before I could even react, a hornet stung me on my lower lip, which swelled instantly larger than a plum. The plane was loaded with servicemen returning home during World War II, and unfortunately, all were killed. I felt so sad and thought a lot about those servicemen losing their lives when they were on their way home after fighting for our country in the war. It also troubled me to learn that people stole personal possessions from the dead soldiers, whose bodies were strewn over several miles in our rural countryside.

Attending the World's Fair was a big eye-opener for me as a nine-year-old. I viewed large miniature landscape exhibits with tiny round futuristic automobiles driving on freeways with cloverleaf on and off ramps. There were fast trains called rockets speeding quickly across the country. Another exhibit had model telephones with television screens so people could view their callers as they were talking on the telephone. I was enthralled and excited about the possible futuristic inventions. There were large exhibits with television screens showing movies, live news broadcasts, and announcers who were reporting world events. This was, of course, at least six or seven years prior to the actual introduction of television for the public, but it seemed that I had a peek into the future about which none of my classmates had any knowledge. This may have given me an advantage when it came to creative possibility thinking. I would definitely need this attribute in my future career.

Freleigh's daughter was younger than I was, and I'm quite sure that it must have been my idea to go exploring, but she knew where there was a thick forest where we could go hiking. We ventured about three blocks from their home, found the trail that she knew about and followed it for a couple of hours, and returned home a little later than either of our parents wanted. But to everyone's shock and dismay, I was covered with red welts which began itching violently and spreading over my entire body. Yes, this was my first but not my last experience with poison ivy. I found out that I was extremely allergic to poison ivy, but she was not and she didn't have any reaction at all. There's nothing like the embarrassment of getting someone else into trouble and then suffering the consequences myself in such an obvious display of red welts. I learned a big lesson that day.

The Freleigh family met together every morning before breakfast, read verses from the Bible, talked about the meaning of the verses, and then each one took a turn praying out loud. Participating in their family devotions made a big impression on me. Our family did not have any such practices, and their family seemed very sincere and authentic in their trust and devotion while reading and praying. They actually were talking and communicating with God. It was easy to sense the genuineness of their relationship with God, whom they called their Heavenly Father, and to see how they entrusted everything in their lives to His divine guidance. Obviously, they were sacrificing everything in their homeland of America in order to build and develop new churches in South America, where they spent many years as missionaries. I respected and admired them very much. I wondered what it was like for their children to attend school in South America, where the teachers and children did not speak English.

The news about the war was on the radio every single day. We wondered if the war would ever be over. I had braces on my teeth for nearly a year when suddenly my orthodontist was drafted and sent to war. My braces had to be removed prior to his departure because there wouldn't be an orthodontist in our area. Unfortunately, the only alternative was to make a trip to Des Moines for appointments with an orthodontist there, but the distance was too great, and the expense could not even be considered. Therefore, my teeth gradually became slightly crooked again and remained that way until I had them corrected well into my sixties. Also, my cousin Bill Kellogg, Oliver's oldest son, enlisted in the navy at that time. His dad, my uncle Oliver, had enlisted in the army earlier in the war and had completed service by the time Bill enlisted; and it was very difficult for him to see his son heading into harm's way. Another son, my cousin Marvin, later enlisted, so their family had a father and two sons in World War II. As time passed, the third son, Edward, served in the Cold War, and Bill served in the Army National Guard in the Vietnam era. We always thought that our servicemen looked very handsome in their uniforms. It became popular to wear navy-type outfits especially for the girls. I remember the cute navy blue dresses with white bias-tape trim which looked like the sailor uniforms. Soon, many of my older cousins and friends were being drafted into the army. Many soldiers were killed in World War II. I did not personally know anyone who was killed, even though there were articles in our local newspaper, the *Globe Gazette*, every day regarding the status of the war and concerning soldiers from our city who were being injured or killed.

During the war, we found out that men were recruited from Germany to replace and assist on family farms where one or more of the sons had been drafted and were serving overseas. This must have been kept very quiet since most of us never knew this was happening until many years later. Now we recognize why there was such a large population of German descendants living in Iowa. These men were most surely prisoners of war known as POWs. When Bill, my cousin, was just out of high school and waiting to join the navy, he worked in a canning factory in Wisconsin with many German and Italian POWs. He stated that many such POWs liked the United States so much that they returned postwar and became citizens.

Phyllis 9, Peggy 5,
Nancy 3

And

Wilbur and Dorothy Kellogg
with daughters Nancy 9,
Peggy 11, Phyllis 16

CHAPTER 4

FAMILY, FRIENDS, AND RELATIVES

The Winnebago River flowed about a mile away from our home, but Lime Creek, a small tributary of that river, surrounded an island behind our home on Crescent Drive. This island about five acres in size was a great attraction for our family and many friends. When we were between five and ten years old, boys loved to go and visit and enjoy hours of exploring the forested island which was alive with wildlife. Catching crawdads, butterflies, snails, minnows, or garter snakes was very exciting. My cousin Russell helped me catch about ten baby garter snakes one day, and it was his idea to place them in a small box and take them door-to-door through our neighborhood to see if we could sell them. Our sales skills were obviously lacking as we really were unable to sell a single snake. Other friends merely enjoyed the sport of finding the snakes, maybe playing with them for a while, and then returning them to their wild habitat. Fifty years later, I returned to see for myself if the natural forested island was still as beautiful and inviting as it was years ago. Amazingly, the island looked the same, heavily overgrown with brush, trees, and wild bushes and berries. The small tributary which used to be about three feet wide and ten feet lower than our backyard had now become a river approximately fifty feet wide and only about one foot lower than our same backyard. Our little home probably had been sold many times and had many different families living there during the past sixty-five years, but it still looks as well kept and new as it did the day when we moved there in 1935. One of my little friends, Jerry Bailey, would ride his tricycle the nearly six blocks to play at our house. Later he became an accomplished concert pianist in Chicago but died at an early age of a heart attack. Visiting his home when I was a child was like taking a trip to a museum. His parents had arranged a large upstairs recreational room for all his unusual toys including glass-encased doll houses, miniature toy soldiers, electric trains, and beautiful stuffed animals. Another friend, Jerry Parks, also enjoyed coming over and hiking with me through the wooded island. That little forested island and the many times we went hiking there will always be a vivid memory permanently framed in my mind.

Rene Wolf was a pretty Jewish girlfriend of mine with whom I would walk home from school every day. Many times, we would stop in at her little brick home for a short visit. Her mother would invite me in and offer me some kosher food as a snack before I would continue walking another six blocks to my home. Rene's family was a very strict Orthodox Jewish family. She would tell me many of the customs which her family followed. I never quite understood the full meaning of their tradition and customs. We were only six or seven years old, and as she patiently explained their customs, I was not quite sure that even she understood what she was trying to tell me. I do know that her father owned a large furniture store in our city and that they were considered to be rich. I also know that she and her mother traveled to California for a couple of months on vacation. Rene looked so happy when she returned. I wondered what it would be like to take a vacation to California not knowing that someday I would live there.

Then there was my closest little friend, Sue Flickinger, who lived a half a block away in a very stately brick home which was beautifully landscaped with rows of flowers adorning the curved brick walkway to the arched vine-covered entrance to her home. Her father was a doctor, and everything in her home was very prim and proper. When she answered the telephone, she would speak with wonderful expression, saying, "Hello, this is the Dr. Flickinger residence, and this is Sue speaking. May I help you?" Many times, I was asked to join their family for their evening meals. I was very impressed by their exquisite manners and politeness. I secretly wished that my family could be so polite and have such polished and meticulous manners.

Pheasant and rabbit hunting as well as muskrat trapping were favorite activities which I shared with my father. Learning to shoot a rifle at the age of ten was a great accomplishment for me. I became an accurate shot and retained that skill throughout my life, which often embarrassed more accomplished marksmen. I had been told and was always well aware that my father wanted a son more than anything else in the world, but having three daughters meant that he would inherently want to teach one of his daughters the skills which he would have desired to have taught a son. Trapping for muskrats meant long and cold trampling or hiking adventures along crooked rivers in the deep crunchy snow. We would set the traps late in the evening and then venture out in the cold morning, often below zero, to find the muskrats which had become entrapped. The fur skins were quite valuable at that time and the fur trader always looked forward to our skins. We would hope for six or eight muskrats per night; however, we usually were only able to deliver four to six skins, and the payment would be somewhere between ten to fifty dollars. We even read about and considered the possibility of raising mink or chinchillas on our farm and selling their skins; however, that idea never materialized.

Winter sports and fun in the snow were high on our list of activities for afterschool, Saturday, or Sunday afternoon parties. We built snow forts and castles, built ski jumps at the bottom of the hill, and loved tobogganing with our friends. We ice-skated frequently on the Winnebago River near our home, and often on Saturday night, we would skate at the East Park ice skating rink, where the music made skating more fun. I learned to twirl and skate backward and to skate as a couple with different friends. We learned to waltz on skates and generally considered skating much like dancing on ice. Often our whole Sunday-school class scheduled skating or tobogganing parties. Refreshments consisting of homemade brownies and hot chocolate milk with marshmallows would always be ready and waiting after our fun in the snow.

During my early teens, I had four or five different sets of friends: the twelve girlfriends from the Alliance Church, three friends from my neighborhood on Crescent Drive, six new friends from the Radio Chapel where we occasionally attended church, a dozen close friends from Jefferson School as well as many cousins and friends who lived on nearby farms in our rural area. By the time I entered junior high school, I was so busy entertaining and spending weekends and overnights with my friends that it seemed I was hardly ever home. Consequently, I scarcely knew my younger sisters. By the time they were entering junior high school, I was already attending Iowa State Teachers College in Cedar Falls, Iowa. I never lived at home again after age seventeen.

Ninth grade began in a very serious way. I loved studying algebra and Latin. It was proving to be my best year yet; however, in November I became very ill and was admitted to Mercy Hospital. Again, this illness came about before antibiotics were available, and my fever raged between 105 and 106. Our family doctor gave no hope for recovery. He diagnosed my illness as polio but had no way of proving what my illness was. A guest evangelist had come to town during that week, and he was scheduled to preach in the Radio Chapel that evening. He was meeting our minister, Rev. Carl Sentman, in his office to discuss the evening service when my severe illness was mentioned to him at about 1:30 p.m. that afternoon. Later I found out that at the exact same time when those two ministers paused in the middle of their discussions and prayed for me to be healed, I was, in fact, healed. I was able to overhear our family doctor, Dr. Eggloff, in the hallway in the hospital (he was an atheist) sarcastically telling my mother that with the exception of a miracle from God, there was nothing else they could do. He instructed the nurse to pull the shades in my room and basically said "Let her go peacefully."

At one thirty, I felt the fever suddenly disappear. I sat up, felt well and strong, and called for the nurse and Dr. Eggloff, telling them that I was well and ready to go home. The doctor was shocked and said with a little less sarcasm, "This has to be a miracle of God, but we need to keep you here for several days for observation to make sure. It's not possible to get well this quick." But it was a fact. I was well again. It was only later that day I learned about the ministers who prayed for my instant healing at exactly 1:30 p.m. I was released from the hospital the next morning and was able to return to school the next day as if I had never been sick at all. I did have to drop my Latin class since the pace of learning new vocabulary was so fast it was almost impossible to catch up. Algebra was a cinch for me, and I did study hard in order to make good grades.

CHAPTER 5

RELIGIOUS INFLUENCES

"Let the children come to me" is a quote from the words of Jesus. Most people never realize that young children are very cognizant of what is expected of them, nor do they realize how much children can assimilate and learn. Actually, in my own work with children, I find that as soon as they are treated in an equal manner, they will rise to the occasion. Research has shown that the human brain has reached full size by age five; therefore, I tell children that even though their body appears small in size compared to that of adults, they can actually think as well as an adult does if they will simply try. I pondered deeply about the Bible stories that were told when I attended Sunday school as early as age three and four. I can remember thinking about many of the little stories throughout the week, wondering about David and Goliath, Noah and the Ark, Jonah and the Whale, the Tower of Babel, and others. We attended the Christian and Missionary Alliance church in Mason City, and the goal of that church was for every single young person to eventually become a missionary somewhere in the world. This emphasis was so instilled in us that every young person was absolutely expected to attend St. Paul Bible Institute after graduating from high school. Anyone who did not fit that pattern was automatically considered to be rebellious against God. Emphasis, I believe, should probably have been placed on the importance of living an exemplary Christian life in whatever career one chose. There were certain amounts of guilt which many of us had to overcome throughout our life if we chose to do anything other than become a missionary.

Guest missionaries and evangelists probably made a greater impact on my thinking and my life than our regular local ministers and Sunday-school teachers did. Perhaps they were more intense in their presentations or motivational in their approach, but I can to this day remember many of the topics and important points of their presentations, messages, or sermons.

Our family began attending a different church in the 1940s, which allowed me an opportunity to have an additional new group of new teenage friends. The new church was called Radio Chapel, and it was very modern in appearance. Inside the high ceiling was curved and dark blue with stars, which were little lights shining exactly as if you were looking at the night sky. There were controls for the lighting which could allow the whole auditorium to look as if it were sunrise, sunset, or the middle of the night. The seats were comfortable, upholstered in dark navy blue mohair material, and would fold up when they weren't in use and would be folded down when someone sat in them. Our former church had long wooden benches which were hard to sit in for long hours. The outside of this building was pure white, rectangular shaped with a curved roof. Rev. Carl Sentman was the minister and he was very personable and involved with everyone in all kinds of church activities.

It was during an evening service at the Radio Chapel when a guest missionary from Africa was speaking that I really began to listen and understand what it meant to become a Christian. I was nine years old at the time, but I understood fully well that I needed to make this very important commitment, which would last for my whole lifetime. I indicated my desire by raising my hand, and an older couple in the church invited me to a room near the front stage, where they prayed with me. I instantly felt a sense of belonging as if God had become my very own Heavenly Father, almost as if an adoption had taken place. My perception that Jesus had already paid the price to erase my sinful nature, which allowed me to receive eternal life, was very clear. The missionary in his sermon likened salvation to a train ticket which was given to me. If I accepted it, I could take the trip; but if I didn't accept it, I would not be able to get onboard. It wasn't that I believed that I had been a bad person but that all people are born with a sinful nature and Jesus died to take away that sinful nature for each person who would believe Him and accept His gift of salvation. This was the first time I understood the plan of salvation which had been written for us in the book of John in the Bible which I could easily quote: "For God so loved the world, that He gave His only begotten Son, that whosoever believeth in Him should not perish, but have eternal life" (John 3:16). My life changed dramatically. Every day thereafter, I felt a sense of God's presence. Everywhere I went, everything I did or said seemed to be flooded with a glowing presence. Talking with God seemed to permeate my thoughts. I began to have a great concern and to feel an inward responsibility for my friends and people everywhere in the world who would also need to have such a transforming experience if they just knew how to or were willing to accept this ticket which we call salvation. It seemed so simple, profound, exhilarating, supernatural, and everlasting. At that young age I began to understand why skeptics were so resentful, hateful, and possibly even jealous. Nothing else that they try in life can give them such a connection to God. Living a good life and doing good deeds simply will not do the trick. Mrs. Hartman was only the first of many such encounters which I would have in my life with people who believed that Christians were haughtily trying to claim a corner on religion, believing theirs was the only way to heaven, the truth being that a person who had a personal experience such as I had would instantly desire for everyone in the world to receive the same gift, which is offered to all. The only prerequisite for receiving this gift is the humbling effort of reaching out and accepting the gift, which is exactly what critics refuse to do. What would they have to lose? The only thing that I think a person could lose would be their pride of wanting to live life in their own way, not God's way.

Another big influence in my life was attending summer Bible camps. It was fortunate, indeed, that even though our family had very limited financial resources, a very high priority was placed on sending me to summer camps. Our biggest church camps were held at Medicine Lake, Minnesota, which was approximately 150 miles from our home. I was able to get a ride to the camp with other families in our church. The campground was rustic, with log cabins, but also with a huge meeting room large enough to seat nearly a thousand people. It was situated on the shores of beautiful Medicine Lake. Attendance ranged around a thousand teenagers, including some of their families, ministers, counselors, and teachers. I well remember trying to convince two other teenagers who were very rebellious against God, faith, and their parents that they should really consider how important it would be for them to become Christians. Ultimately, they did respond and decided to make the decision to become Christians. It was meaningful for me to observe firsthand how the lives of both of those girls changed from having horribly negative attitudes against everyone and everything into instant radiant, loving, caring personalities in just one night and only after making the decision to accept God's gift to them.

While attending camp at Medicine Lake during the summer of 1947, I personally met Billy Graham and his wife, Ruth. They were very dedicated. They went to the chapel each morning at 6:00 a.m. to pray for more than an hour every single day. Their friends, Cliff Barrows and George Beverly Shea, were also there. Billy Graham preached at our evening services that week. He was dynamic and gave a clear message. George Beverly Shea sang with his marvelous baritone voice. Later on toward the end of our week at camp, Billy Graham announced that they felt that God wanted them to organize an Evangelistic Gospel Crusade. Billy Graham would preach, George Beverly Shea would sing, and Cliff Barrows would make the announcements and direct the audience singing as well as become the business manager. They planned to schedule their first crusade in the Los Angeles area in the fall of 1947. It has been rewarding to attend several of Billy Graham's crusades over the years and to follow the news of his successful ministry even until now after he has retired.

By the time I was seventeen, I was asked to teach a summer daily vacation Bible school class in a nearby school in Central Heights. We had moved again for about the eighth time. I didn't know any friends or neighbors near this farm, so I was willing to take on a new opportunity. This was my first experience in teaching, and I felt that I was able to make a noticeable difference in the lives of those children. The children listened, and I had a surge of feelings of success and felt that I could become a successful teacher.

Music played an important part in influencing my Christian belief system. When I was only five years old, my parents purchased a Wurlitzer Spinet piano which was forty-two inches high, exactly the same as my height at that time. I took piano lessons weekly from age five until my second year of college. I also took voice lessons but discontinued singing in my late twenties. Later in life, I realized that music seemed to leave indelible impressions on the minds of children. That was the reason that I later wrote phonics lessons and set the lessons to music for children in the public schools. Later in life, I noticed that when I taught songs to students, even to groups of a hundred or more at a time, the students were able to recall the musical lyrics and words three and four years later; but when I labored to teach phonics to the same students, they were rarely able to recall any of their lessons, whether days, weeks, or months later. Music used as a natural teaching technique has been long ignored but can be utilized to more effectively teach phonics, math, science, or other lessons with a greater percentage of retention.

Singalongs were always popular. A large organization called Youth for Christ was very popular during my teenage years. Attending such meetings on Friday nights was a great place for teenagers to gather as well as a great outing for those special dates. These meetings were basically singalongs with brief messages of inspiration, admonishments, and testimonies regarding spiritual life experiences from young people. We even added singalongs to our home activities and invited our friends and other teenagers to come over for evenings of singing and refreshments. Cherry cobblers, chocolate or melted brown sugar, coconut frosting on a unique yellow butter hot milk cake recipe which my mother often baked were favorites. My parents purchased one of the very first recording devices, called a wire recorder; and we enjoyed recording our group singing, talking, and laughing together on these special occasions. We also took turns visiting and having singing parties in homes of cousins and friends, where I was invited to accompany their singing on the piano. Having taken piano lessons from the early age of five, I not only played almost every hymn by heart, but I could also read the music and play the piano for a few popular songs. Nearly all the songs which we sang for hours were church hymns, favorite choruses, and other old-time favorites.

Needless to say, the churches which our family attended were very conservative. We were never allowed to see a movie as that was considered to be worldly and we might be exposed to ideas of which the church would not approve. The only movie that was approved and which we were able to see was *The King of Kings*. Playing cards or listening to a radio soap-opera program would also be disallowed. The radio program, *Henry Aldrich*, was often the highlight of the week. I listened to *Inner Sanctum* once, and it was so scary that I must have had nightmares for a week. Certainly, life was busy enough for me without those things, but I did feel at a disadvantage when my classmates and friends in school were attending Shirley Temple, Donald Duck, and whatever other popular movies came to town. On the other hand, we had our own movie camera, and ample time was spent taking and sharing our own family movies with friends and family. I do remember, however, visiting one of our church families in their home where they showed the Laurel and Hardy movies and some cartoons. I'm not certain, to this day, if our opinions on life might have been different had we attended movies in the movie theater like everyone else did; but I do know that when I was in my first year of teaching school, I attended a real movie in a theater, and besides feeling somewhat guilty, I couldn't see that there had been any harm done. When I mentioned attending a movie when speaking to my father on the phone, the news was met with great dismay.

CHAPTER 6

PROGRESSIVE CLUB

T he history of the Progressive Club probably goes back to the late 1890s, but the earliest recollections which I have were when my grandmother Gertrude Bauer was the president. She was organized, efficient, personable, intelligent, and a second-generation teacher. She led the club through many innovative ventures such as quilting parties, potluck evenings, talent shows, Christmas programs, holiday celebrations, work parties, and talent-scout programs. Progressive Club meetings were held once a month at the home of a designated member, and the attendance usually was between sixty to seventy-five people. Memorizing a long poem at Christmas when I was three and reciting it in front of this group was one of my earliest public presentations. There were many to follow; however, I guess I had to start somewhere. I do remember early renditions of what is now called karaoke, which were performed by two neighboring farm girls. They played music on a record and were literally able to mimic the music and expressions of the recording artists that were popular in the 1930s and 1940s. I thought they were extremely talented. I'm not sure, but I do believe that they must have gone on into successful musical or acting careers.

My grandfather Bauer had been secretary on the board for the electrical company which installed the very first electrical poles and wiring in the country east of Mason City, Iowa, which would connect the Bauer farm and their neighbors for electricity in 1905. I still have the original book of minutes for those important meetings. His handwriting was impeccably done in cursive script. I loved my grandfather a lot, but I did not have the opportunity to become very well acquainted since we lived in St. Paul at that time. He died suddenly with a heart attack after trying to push our neighbor Mabel Pippert's car when she had car trouble. That was the second time during a big snowstorm that he had helped her with her car during that storm. My grandfather pushed her car both times to get it started again. I was only three but was well aware of the emotions of my mother and grandmother regarding his untimely death. My mother always believed that she had been favored by her father because he trusted her to drive his new 1920 Model T Ford, chauffeuring her older brother and sister and a couple of cousins to school when she was only ten years old. When in her nineties she recalled several other instances, confirming his idolizing her as a special daughter. Her older sister, Wilma, was thought to have been a genius in all aspects. She lived only into her early twenties and allegedly died from an attempted abortion, leaving her two young toddlers, Robert and Russell Brown, to be raised and adopted by her mother, my grandmother Bauer. The father of these boys, Steve Brown, was an alcoholic who had wandered from his family, his whereabouts usually unknown.

Times changed dramatically upon the death of Arthur Bauer, but the Progressive Club went forward. Perhaps the leadership in the community kept Gertrude active and politically involved. Neighbors, friends, and family looked to Gertrude for strength, financial support, and leadership; however, the financial resources began to wane. Wilma's sons, when older, probably were not as resourceful or qualified to manage the Bauer estate as was hoped. Additionally, Gertrude's youngest son, Kenneth, was more interested in his boxing career, breaking colts for the rodeo, and in bull riding than he was in managing a business. He seemed to be always sporting one or another new injury. There were rumors that he was possibly leaning on his mother in order to advance his own interests. This was not an easy situation to understand. Gertrude appeared gullible; and while obviously favoring Kenneth, these situations strained her to the limit, and I believe these may have been the underlying reason for the sudden termination of the Kellogg Dairy Business, which my father had propelled into such a successful business. No one will ever know.

CHAPTER 7

EARLY EDUCATION

The first three and a half years of my elementary school education were spent at Wilson Elementary School in Mason City, Iowa. This school was one of the designated and distinguished teacher-training schools where student teachers from Iowa State Teachers College from Cedar Falls, Iowa, were assigned to complete their student-teaching requirements in order to qualify for their teaching credentials. Iowa State Teachers College ranked second only to the renowned Columbia University in the east. The teacher-training courses in this college were extremely innovative and advanced. Other colleges appeared to be inadequate in teacher-preparation courses as happens in California I was to find out later. At any rate, the latest technology, with the exception of computer classes, seemed to be utilized in that educational program nearly sixty-five years ago. More recently, research has indicated that teachers revert to teaching in the same manner as they were originally taught when attending elementary school themselves rather than utilizing what they learned in college. Exemplary teachers definitely assisted me in the formation of my teaching style and techniques. This turned out to be extremely advantageous to my future career in teaching and the administration of both public and private schools.

One organizational concept which was implemented during those early years was the idea of outlining or organizing the entire day during the first few minutes of class time. For example, the teacher would begin to write the time schedule for the day but include ideas from the class regarding what needed to be learned and how much time each subject or project might take. This time schedule of mini goals to reach was left on the chalkboard for reference, revision, or even review at the end of the day, when each item was considered as to whether it had been accomplished or needed to be continued to the following day. This constant internal planning and making a check list daily, whether mentally or written, has become a valuable and a very intrinsic tool throughout my life. It is a fact that if a person sets a goal or writes down a list of everything that needs to be accomplished, he or she will have a greater chance of reaching those goals. It is my opinion that anyone who lacks goals and direction will merely drift through life, have a tendency to become lazy and disoriented, and feel worthless. The same is true in the classroom. Minutes, hours, and days are lost as teachers neglect to involve their students in goal-oriented learning. Additionally, when people allow others to direct their time and their life, they lose control over their time and their personal goals. Turning on the television and letting the programs dictate what will happen for the next hour or more or letting friends or family set the agenda for the day, week, or year without any personal input into the process are ways to lose control, waste time, and begin letting life drift into mediocrity. This idea should be a cause for a "no life left behind" campaign.

Creativity was inspired in me while attending elementary school. It is amazing what children can do when their expressions of writing, drawing, painting, or acting are respected. The grading system as currently utilized to place every child at some point on a bell-shaped curve has been detrimental to creativity, I believe. If that same critical measurement were given to the first words uttered by a toddler, I doubt that children would want to learn to talk. Speech seems to be accepted no matter how feeble the first attempts whereas in school, every stroke of the crayon or pencil is met with critical judgment. Yes, we want every child to succeed with no child left behind; but consider the negative, lackadaisical educational atmosphere which most children encounter in the public-school systems today. Testing once or twice a year in order to determine if a child is learning is not the answer and certainly is not enough. Unless a teacher is able to bring out the best in each child and guide each child in self-motivation, and self-actualization, it is hardly possibly to push any child to become well educated. Pushing a child or a group of children will be met with resistance, a wall, or mechanisms of self-defense and then self-denial. Testing is an important part of teaching but must happen after each and every introduction of a new concept. That is the point at which no child should be left behind. More often than not, teachers seem to continue on throughout the year with lesson after lesson; and if only one or two children understand each concept, the teacher seems to continue on toward the next lesson in the book regardless of how many students are left behind. It is this accumulation of being left behind that eventually overwhelms a child and then creates a tendency for that student to give up or become a dropout.

Fortunately, in my early educational experiences, every single child counted; and every single concept had to be mastered there on the spot. Memorization was important, and if multiplication tables were to be learned, then they were to be mastered by every single child no matter what it took. Speed and accuracy were important. Counting on fingers was not taught or allowed. These facts were to be indelibly enshrined in the brain. Proper penmanship was not only taught, but meticulous handwriting was also required. Proper posture was not ignored but was an absolute requirement for every student every day. The art of manuscript or penmanship did not just happen in the early years of the history of our country; it was required and adhered to with pride.

Traveling extensively throughout the world over a period of about ten years looking for exemplary educational models led me to understand why our schools in America are lagging behind. When visiting schools in the countries of Japan, Taiwan, China, or Russia, I never observed such a relaxed, unproductive daily educational schedule as which exists every single day in our American schools. Not only are the public-school days and school years shorter in America, but the actual minutes of intensive instruction are also almost nonexistent. The hours spent watching television, educational videos, playing computer-type games, recess, recreation, and relaxation far outweigh any instructional time in our public schools. Additionally, high expectations on the part of parents regarding the educational accomplishments of their child are generally absent. Parents, in general, can be easily duped into believing that their child is doing well in school by merely seeing good grades on their report card and never hearing about any possible learning or discipline problems.

Parents in general really do not want to be bothered with anything that happens in school if that is possible. The educational system in America, with only a few exceptions, is understandably next to the lowest in the world. It is often referred to as the "dumbing" down of America simply because each generation of parents become more lax and less educated. Granted there are a few highly motivated students who rise up to take leadership or governmental-type positions, but they are definitely in the minority. Most Americans settle for eight-to-five jobs and hope they will have enough money to retire on when they reach age sixty or sixty-five. Increasingly more Americans want the government to provide their employment, health care, retirement, housing, care, and education of their children. There seems to be little incentive to work hard and start a business, partially due to the fact that taxes are so high, the responsibility great, and working that hard leaves very little time, if any, for their highest priority, which is usually fun, and pleasure.

CHAPTER 8

FRIENDS AND COMRADES

Friends play an important part in the development of a person's personality. Developing relationships and learning how to get along with others are probably among the most important forces in the world. Relationships can be fragile. Throughout biblical times as well as all during subsequent recorded history, it seems that human beings have had trouble getting along with each other. There have been wars and rumors of wars ever since Cain and Abel fought and Cain finally killed Abel.

The desire of American people during the last hundred years has always been their quest for peace in the world. What is it that hinders people from getting along? Why must there be arguments, differences of opinion, and political strategies to take over the world? Must the last days as prophesied in the book of Revelation in the Bible really come true? Are there no alternatives? Will the terrorists strike again? Will everyone live in fear from now until the end of time? These are the questions in the minds of most people.

My family treasured friends and friendship. Friends were always welcome in our home. My parents went out of their way to celebrate everyone's birthday, anniversary, birth of a child, graduation, and any other celebration they heard about. Family reunions were important events. Some of our early family reunions were held at least a hundred miles from our home at a park high on the banks of the Mississippi River. Relatives came from long distances and brought their favorite casseroles, meats, salads, and desserts for a huge potluck picnic. As youngsters from the ages eight to maybe eighteen, we would spend the afternoon exploring the nearby hills and caves. There was one large cave which we entered where we found veins and layers of sandstone of nearly every color in the rainbow. We hurried back to the picnic area and found jars and containers and some tools for scraping, and then we returned to the cave as fast as we could. We scratched the damp sandstone loose and placed different colors in the jars, forming unique artistic designs in the jar as we alternated putting in different colors of sand. The sand was already naturally moist from the dampness in the cave. We had to be careful to pack the sand firmly, seal the lid tightly, and place our jars where they would dry fairly quickly; otherwise, mildew would grow in the sand. My colorful jar was used as a decorative paper weight for many years.

There eventually was a real tragedy in the Kellogg family. My cousin Martha was the first one in our family to actually experience a serious tragedy when her son Kelly was struck by a train and killed instantly. He had tried to follow his mother on his bike as she was driving to the grocery store. Her grief was only comforted by turning to God and her belief that Kelly would be in heaven, where she would see him again someday. Her spiritual life was greatly strengthened as she endured the deep grief from the loss of her only son. One other tragedy struck the Kellogg family when my cousin Roy was working for a logging company near their home in Wisconsin. He was guiding logs down the river, balancing on the slippery logs when he accidently fell into the river, was trapped under the logs, and pulled down by an undercurrent. His drowning was so very unexpected and unfortunate.

Over the years there seemed to be what we now refer to as "cross-generational" communication amongst family members, much more so than in our current generation. We became close friends and very well acquainted with our grandparents, aunts, and uncles and other older relatives, discussing ideas, feelings, their pasts, and their hopes and dreams for the future. This aspect of communication seems to be nonexistent now. Currently, it seems that adult children expect their parents and grandparents to "babysit" their young children or care for them while they enjoy their social life. Furthermore, today, children expect to be constantly entertained or given gifts. If the children say thank you or write a personal thank-you note, that is considered sufficient communication between the child and the grandparent to last for the full year or until the next gift is given. Parents as well as grandparents structure whatever little time they have together by taking the children to a movie, shopping, or to an amusement park. If unable to take the children somewhere "exciting," the next best thing seems to be to watch television, a video, or a DVD. In other words, children expect to be entertained, and parents and grandparents are not expected to be worthy of genuine heartfelt communication or sharing of real feelings. There is almost no communication on a deeper level than a mere hello or thank you. Young people seem uninterested in how you are getting along or what might be happening in your life say nothing about learning about their many experiences in life. They seem to want to find out what movie they can see next, what video game they can play, what messages they can text to or receive from their friends, or what they can arrange to do without parents or grandparents being involved. Perhaps Walt Disney had some influence in this aspect since visiting Disneyland seems to be the ultimate entertainment which a parent can give a child. That type of entertainment seems to take precedence over other more intimate types of social activities such as discussions about their lives, current events, spiritual growth, games, camping, traveling, or singing together.

The next observation that I have about American children is that they seem to only want to communicate exclusively with other children, whether in their own family, age group, clique, or club. There is a real airy attitude among most young people in that they want exclusivity to their chosen group. The close family structures seem to be disappearing as well as community loyalty, respect for our American flag, our president, and government leaders.

CHAPTER 9

FARMING AS A WAY OF LIFE

Farmers who lived in the country in the early 1930s seemed to depend on their ability to provide a living for their family from the land they owned. They also depended on assistance from other farm friends and neighbors who would help them when the crops were ready to be planted or harvested. There were also big canning-work days when fruits and vegetables needed to be preserved for the long winter months. The women and children were all expected to help with picking apples from the trees and then bringing in the pumpkins, squash, and other vegetables from the gardens. Cucumbers were made into pickles; grapes were made into juice or sometimes into wine. Nonetheless, there was a big community effort to get ready for the winter months. Oftentimes, certain vegetables could be stored in a cellar which had an outside entrance and would be very cold all winter. These vegetables would have to be covered with sawdust so they would stay cold but not freeze. All perennial bulbs had to be dug up, covered with saw dust, and placed in the cellar for storage during the winter months. Seeds were gathered from flowers such as sunflowers, daisies, and hollyhocks for storage until the spring. Mothers and grandmothers had quilting parties so they could make enough quilts to keep their families warm during the cold winter months. Wood had to be chopped or enough coal delivered to last for the entire winter. The cistern had to be cleaned and kept full so there would be sufficient rainwater to last until the melting snow and spring rains would fill it again. The cistern in my grandmother's house was a concrete room as a section of the basement where the walls came up to within two feet of the basement ceiling. The cistern had to be checked periodically to rid it of anything that might contaminate the water. Rainwater or melting snow drained into the cistern from the rain gutters on the roof. Occasionally a bird or a mouse might accidentally fall into the water. One day I even heard a pitiful howling from the cistern, and when I went to the basement, I found that one of our baby kittens had fallen into the water. She was so fearful of drowning that she was scratching violently in her attempt to get out. I was able to save the kitten's life, and I don't think the kittens ever went near the cistern again after that experience.

There are four distinct seasons in the Midwest, and each is met with excitement and a lot of work. Spring is a time for preparing the soil and planting crops. The first outing each spring for our family was a picnic to Bluebell Island. This little island about ten miles from our home was covered with wild bluebell plants. They were the very first plant to bloom in the spring. The flowers are shaped like bells with several bluebells hanging from each stem. Everything must be done in a timely manner in the spring. The soil must be dry enough from the heavy winter snow so the tractors or horses won't get stuck; however, one should not wait too long, or it would be too dry for the seeds to sprout and the growing season would not be long enough before harvesttime because the cold winds come quickly in the fall. Additionally, in the spring we would carefully lift one or more baby robins from their nest just a day or two before they were ready to fly. We hand-fed them an egg custard, and we dug up worms for them. Baby robins were tamed easily and they would stay close with us for several weeks before they would venture out into the world by themselves. They would stand on our shoulders or nearby us as we worked or played. They readily flew to us whenever we called "Rob-ee." Caring for one or two baby robins each spring was like a hobby for our family.

Summers are warm and humid and alive with insects. This is a time to enjoy the beauty of the land, watch the crops grow, and use a spray on the crops if the insects were trying to overtake them. Early summer was also a time when weeds had to be pulled in the fields. The tractor was able to cultivate rows of corn and beans, but pulling out mustard plants had to be done by hand. We were paid one penny for pulling out ten complete mustard plants and their entire roots. One hundred plants would be worth ten cents, and we had to pull one thousand mustard plants in order to earn one dollar. Those were long, hard working days for us as children. When summer came, it was also a time for swimming and boating at nearby Clear Lake, summer camps for kids and families, picnics, riding horseback, rodeos, and the county fair. We were always able to make time to play after all the work was done. The 4-H club friends of mine spent spring and summer preparing animals, fruits, vegetables, sewing, and baking items for the exhibits which they entered for judging at the county fair.

Autumn comes quickly, school sessions begin, and harvesting was always a rush time. The weather is known to change quickly, and weather reports in those days were only erratically accurate and mostly anybody's guess. We learned to study and understand the clouds and changing winds, but we could still be easily caught off guard by a sudden thunderstorm that might flatten a whole field of corn, wheat, or oats prior to harvesting. That actually happened to our family when a sudden hailstorm battered our field of corn before it was ready to be harvested. The crop was a near total loss, and after we salvaged a few wagonloads, which we picked off the ground by hand, the whole field had to be raked and burned.

Winter snowstorms usually began sometime between Thanksgiving and Christmas. Temperatures could drop to forty below zero, or it could warm up to nearly thirty degrees above zero. Snow could be blown by the winds into drifts that might be ten to fifteen feet deep. These drifts were a severe hazard to cars driving on the narrow two-lane highways, so windbreak fences were built near the sides of the road to trap the snow, causing it to drift prior to reaching the highway. When these large drifts occurred near the trees on our farm, they made wonderful snowbanks for carving out rooms and building snow castles inside the snowbanks. Winters were often long. There were many winter-type jobs to do also. Sidewalks and driveways had to be shoveled. Cows had to be milked twice a day; cattle, horses, pigs, and chickens had to be fed and cared for daily. The barns and pens had to be cleaned, and fresh straw needed to be brought down from the loft and placed in each pen to keep the animals warm and clean. Bales of hay or loose hay needed to be tossed down through the square hole in the floor of the loft for the farm animals to eat. Thinking back, I realize how dangerous it was to work in the loft with two or three open areas in the flooring. One slip on the smooth hay and one would have landed on a concrete floor fifteen feet below. The trees that were dead or damaged had to be cut down and chopped into small-enough logs to fit into the wood furnace or the wood cooking stove. Eventually, we bought coal to burn in the furnace, and the coal would usually burn until the wee early-morning hours. Clothes had to be washed and hung on the clothesline, where they would often freeze before drying. Lest we ever forget, there were those long treks, one hundred feet or more, through the snow to the infamous outhouse. When there were young children in the home, families often improvised with a covered container which was often referred to as a "thunder pot" for the use of the children. Coal and wood for heat was scarce and it could often be thirty to forty degrees inside the house by early morning, so children wore heavy flannel pajamas and maybe as many as five or six blankets or quilts on their beds. It would also be important to wear heavy socks because if one should step on the cold floor, it would almost be like walking outside in the snow.

All in all, life in the Midwest in the early 1930s was still quite primitive. Yes, we had electricity and a country-shared telephone line, outhouses, and a furnace that needed to be stoked and filled with wood or coal every few hours; but we actually had much more family communication, community teamwork, shared times working together, and a sense of having to depend on growing our own food, harvesting, preserving it, and relying on mother nature to help send enough rain for the crops and gardens. No, we did not have a television, cell phone, iPad, iPod, or computer. There was less crime, more caring and sharing by neighbors and friends, and more reliance on families, friends, pastors, and the church. We treasured our family, friends, freedom, and our country. Maybe it wasn't all that bad after all.

CHAPTER 10

THE IMPORTANCE OF ATHLETICS

My father played on his football team when he was in high school during spring and summer, and then he played ice hockey in the winter. He was very athletically inclined and was determined to teach me to become an excellent ice skater. He taught me to skate on the ice rink at the University of Wisconsin at River Falls, Wisconsin, where he had grown up. I was merely three years old but remember entering the warming hut and noticing that I was the only child among all the college students. I became quite an excited skater trying to learn simple routines but nothing like the marvelous skaters with their intricate routines which we see today. Watching international Olympic skating competitions almost always brings back a lot of memories. I believe that I might also have been able to compete if I would really have applied myself and concentrated on that sport. Skiing was another sport that I was expected to learn at the very early age of five. I often see young children skiing on the slopes in Mammoth, Breckenridge, or Keystone. I personally know they can ski as well and as much as they would like at a young age.

Gymnastics seemed to be my favorite sport or pastime. I could do dozens of circles going around the bar with one knee over the bar and holding on with both hands, one hand, and even with no hands at all. I played on the bars practicing a number of tricks every chance I could get. Classmates would often hurry to the bars, sit down on the ground, and watch me do tricks for the whole recess. I was fortunate that I never felt dizzy or tired. No one else in the whole school seemed to want to master tricks on the bars. It was enjoyable to have the opportunity to have so much fun on the bars. Actually, in hindsight, I think that I might have been considered a show-off, but that never entered my mind. I merely enjoyed doing more rotations faster and faster. I could barely wait for recess to come around so that I could have that much fun.

Rope climbing, track, and high jumping were other sports which I enjoyed at Roosevelt Junior High School. Probably I had built up more endurance and skill while working such long hours doing work on the farm. I had often climbed to the top of several of our tall pine trees. One time I had to run very fast across the pasture in order to run away from an old bull that was very angry. I reached the barbed wire fence only split seconds ahead of the bull. Scrambling between the barbed wire strands, I scraped and scarred my right knee, which would always be a reminder to stay away from bulls amongst our cattle.

Horseback riding was probably my most enjoyable sport. A person really must be able to communicate with your horse in order for it to follow your commands. I learned one day while riding a horse that belonged to my uncle Kenneth that you can never let a horse control you or get out from under your control. I had no sooner mounted that horse bareback than it took off running and jumped over a four-foot-high tree stump. He was going to show me that he could do whatever he wanted to do, and therefore, he tried to throw me off by standing up on his back feet and whinnying. I never let a horse think that he could do whatever he wanted to do after that. I learned to be the one who controlled the horse, and then we both could get along very well.

Softball was a popular sport that I played, but I definitely didn't want to spend very much time playing ball. The game "king of the mountain" was another game the children in our neighborhood played. That was a rough game, and I didn't see any big advantage to becoming the king at the top of a high snow mound; but this was a serious game, and the person making it to the top without being knocked down was definitely the champion or the "king of the mountain." Hiking through the woods, pastures, or fields was a great pastime. Bicycling was also popular, but riding on the narrow rural highways which often had no shoulder was dangerous. Bicycling around the farm, going from the house to the barn and/or even out to the pasture was an everyday event. It was always much faster than walking.

Becoming a baton-twirling majorette and marching with the junior high school band was something I really was proud to have accomplished. I recall that in the fall when the weather became quite cold, it was very difficult to hold on to the baton because the metal was so cold and slippery. Somehow we managed and rarely dropped our batons during our performance at halftime for our school football games.

Swimming was taught each year at our junior high school. The pool was nearly Olympic size, and after swimming the required laps, I would spend all of my free swim time learning how to develop a smooth high-diving style. I loved high diving. There were two or three diving boards, but the highest diving board was approximately fifteen feet above the water. There was never enough time to make all the dives that I wanted to make.

CHAPTER 11

MUSIC AS THE SPICE OF LIFE

Music seems to make the world go around, and certainly, it makes a big difference to have music in the air. I can hardly imagine what it would be like if there were no music and if the birds didn't sing.

Meredith Wilson chose his hometown Mason City as the setting for the musical, *The Music Man*. Since then, Music Man Square has been built in Mason City, which depicts the 1912 River City Streetscape as well as a Reunion Hall plus a mini museum containing examples of early musical instruments. The River City Streetscape contains a live size replica of the cobblestone street, including the unique street lanterns from the movie *Music Man*. Candy shops, an ice-cream store, a dress maker shop, a shoe shop, a radio station and a bank have been replicated with additional little shops containing novelty and historical memorabilia from earlier days in Mason City. One of the purposes of the Music Man Square is to provide opportunities for children and people of all ages to learn and perform in the performing arts center. There are lessons available and several practice rooms as well as rooms available for summer musical camps. Meredith Wilson's boyhood home is nearby and is open for tours. Along with the Music Man Square, there are other interesting attractions which bring the heritage of Mason City alive. A short walk to the Mason City Public Library and stroll across the Lime Creek footbridge and one can easily empathize and understand the reasons why Meredith Wilson chose to honor Mason City.

Later in high school, I became completely involved in the music program, traveling to state competitions, singing solos, duets, trios, quartets, in the chorus and as a member of a madrigal group of eight singers. Effie Karamitros in our class was already an accomplished and professional-level pianist who accompanied our choir as well as our madrigal group. She told us that in her home, she was required to practice the piano every evening for five hours, and I found it hard to imagine how she could practice for such long hours. Mr. Paul Nissen, our music director, was very precise in his expectations for each person in the music program. Our high school chorus performed the *Nutcracker Suite*, which was a very difficult arrangement to sing, at Christmas; and our madrigal group was invited to perform at several community functions throughout the school year. I have wondered if Meredith Willson received his musical training from someone as talented as Paul Nissen.

Playing the piano for a few minutes or for hours was something that I always managed to fit into my schedule almost every day. Even though I attended school, had homework, was in charge of feeding and watering the chickens, and driving the tractor on the farm, sometimes for eight hours or more at a time, I still kept up with practicing the piano and singing. Later, in college, I continued taking piano and voice lessons and then additionally choral directing, which would become an important skill for my future plans for teaching children.

CHAPTER 12

TRUTH OR CONSEQUENCES IN DATING

Being around boys really began at the early age of five when boys would call and ask to come to play, hike, and explore the island behind my home. Later after we moved to three different farms east of Mason City, I would frequently get phone calls from boys asking if they could come over and see our new litter of pigs, ride my pony, or just enjoy a few hours of farm life. I never took any of these friendships to mean more than that each boy wanted to experience farm life in the summer and share our toboggan and homemade ski jump in the winter. One can usually see more clearly in hindsight, and now I think I was such a tomboy that boys felt comfortable including me in their activities. We always liked to do the same kind of activities. I was never involved in playing with dolls, working crossword puzzles, playing Monopoly, or going to the movies as other girls seemed to be doing during that period.

My first real date came when my parents took me to visit a Pentecostal church on the other side of town. I was surprised by the display of emotions from the people in the audience. I remember that the guest minister, Rev. Roggow, was from South Dakota, but I remember nothing about his sermon. I was sixteen years old. Walking down the long steps in front of the church after the service, two young men approached me and asked if they could take me out for hot chocolate. As I recall, my answer was no, but they could go and visit our home sometime. Both of the boys were from South Dakota. Mervin, aged eighteen, was the minister's son; and his cousin, Darrell, was twenty-one. Both of them were asking for a date with me. I said that I would arrange for a blind date for one of them. Mervin reluctantly volunteered, and I continued to ponder as to who would be a good blind date for him in order to break up our awkward threesome. I told him that I had a girlfriend who looked enough like me that teachers had mixed us up. I called Beverly, and she was thrilled at the opportunity for a blind date as she had never dated anyone that I knew about. She had two older brothers, Bill and Marvin, but she had never had a serious boyfriend. At any rate, we met for a Saturday-evening ride and drove many miles out into the country. Mervin was driving and speeding on snowy and icy country roads when we approached a ninety-degree turn in the road. Unfortunately, we ended up in a serious automobile crash down into a deep ditch. This happened prior to seat belts. Each of the three of us passengers suffered minor injuries. The most severe injury occurred when Darrell's head struck the light fixture on the ceiling of the car, sending blood splashing everywhere. Hours later in the hospital, after at least forty stitches diagonally across his forehead, we had to call my parents to go and give us a ride to our respective homes. Correspondence with Darrell continued for a few months. At twenty-one years of age, he was pressing very hard to find a wife so that he could marry and avoid being drafted. Mervin and Beverly married the next year, had two sons, and lived happily ever after.

In my life, there were a number of friends who were boys over the next six years. I never took them seriously, but every single one seemed to propose and place pressure on me for sex and marriage. It wasn't easy, but I managed to remain firm and standoffish until after marriage. Certainly, I think I was exposed to nearly all the ploys and tricks which men try to use in order to force the culmination of their desire for sexual gratification. My advice to young girls dating would be to refuse any more than a good-night kiss. Kissing is like a green light to a man on a date, and he could easily overpower someone with less strength.

There is no test that I know of that could be administered to a perspective suitor that would indicate if his real intentions are true or false. I met one of my most persistent suitors when I was seventeen and a guest at an Inter Varsity banquet. Inter Varsity was a nonsectarian religious group which met weekly at Iowa State Teachers College. His name was Dale Henry. He, his cousin Dan Magee, Bill Shaw, and Ellis Tufvander had become acquainted with my mother while she was attending Iowa State Teachers College in Cedar Falls, Iowa, to renew her teaching credentials the prior summer of 1949. I had a summer job detasseling corn just a few miles from my home in Mason City, for a local seed company that summer. I had such a dark tan that my mother, who had not seen me for two months, was visibly embarrassed. She expressed her embarrassment to everyone. Nonetheless, Dale sat next to me at the banquet, and we talked during the evening. Later that evening in the restaurant lobby, an African American college student approached me and inquired as to what percentage of black I was. After explaining that I had been working all summer in the sun and was merely very tan, he strolled away. A girl could be picked up at the slightest hint of eye contact or a smile. After returning home from the banquet, I had no further contact with anyone I had met at that banquet until the following summer when I began my first quarter of college work at that same college.

When I arrived at college for my first quarter, I was surprised to learn that Dale, whom I had met the prior summer, was now completing his last term of college work in order to receiving his bachelor of arts degree. That summer Dale was dating a "pleasingly plump blond girl," as he described her, from the Inter Varsity Group. We nicknamed her Miscellaneous because she was quite emotional, easily jealous, and always wanting to control everyone. He called me and asked me to play a game of miniature golf with him, which I did. There were many repercussions from Miscellaneous and her friends as well as from another of Dale's girlfriends whose name was Florice. She was so upset that I had accepted an invitation to play miniature golf with Dale that she scolded me severely for butting into her relationship with Dale. She married a doctor shortly thereafter, but I never seemed to forget the accusation she made whereby playing one game of miniature golf with Dale had interfered with her relationship with him. During that term, I had a roommate whose name was Bessie, and she was sincerely interested in getting better acquainted with Bill Shaw. One afternoon, Bill called her, asking her for a date that evening. Incidentally, Bill's roommate turned out to be Dale Henry and the two of them connived to set me up with Dale so that we could have dinner together at their apartment and that is exactly what happened. Dale was on the college wrestling team, and soon after the dinner, we returned; and he parked his car in front of my dormitory, jumped out, and immediately demonstrated how he could stand on his head for several minutes. I was actually embarrassed as this seemed unusual, especially since other college students were walking past and looking at him. He graduated in August and moved to a small town in the southwestern part of Iowa to accept a high school teaching position in September of 1950. Bessie subsequently married Bill, after which he accepted a teaching position in Kansas. His first week of teaching would change their lives forever. Traditionally during the first week of school, the teachers would play a softball game against the students, and Bill was struck in the temple by a fly ball and died within hours. I had sung at their wedding, felt very close to them, and was devastated by the news. Bessie years later met and married a widowed minister who had five children. The last I knew they were very happy, and I know she would make a wonderful, caring minister's wife.

I roomed in Bartlett Hall, one of the girls' dormitories, with four other roommates in the fall session. It seemed that we did nothing but study every minute. However, one afternoon when I returned to our room after class, I found my roommates crying and sobbing hysterically. They appeared to be so overcome with emotions that they couldn't tell me anything. Finally, they pointed for me to go and look in another dorm room across the hall from our room. I found one of our classmates sprawled on the floor, covered with blood. I was traumatized with fear; however, it was soon revealed to be a staged prank whereby they had used ketchup all over the bed, floor, and her body. This was a real shocker to those of us who were returning from our classes and didn't know anything about the prank. Those who were involved were really trying to cover their hysterical laughing under their sobs because they were really trying to scare everyone. Scenes like this do happen in real life with much more severe consequences. It did seem as if some action should have been taken to punish them for crying "wolf" when this could actually have been a true murder scene.

Meanwhile, after teaching for only two months Dale was drafted and trained for about three months on base in Fort Campbell, Kentucky. Then he was shipped out from San Francisco, after which he arrived in Korea and was sent to the front lines the next day after his arrival. His first day on the front line in combat was extremely traumatic. He witnessed both of his buddies, one on each side of him, killed by enemy fire. The second day, he was placed on the front line again; however, this time it was he who received shrapnel that pierced his lungs, legs, and groin, for which he was later awarded a purple heart. Later I learned that he was able to drag himself for several miles away from enemy territory and into friendly territory, praying all the while. One lung collapsed, and he was obviously in severe pain. Correspondence moved very slowly, but it was several months before I learned the details of his injury, his hospitalization, and eventually of his assignment to an army office position.

Ninety-nine percent of my dating experiences were what I would term relationships where there were hidden agendas. Not until I would become sixty years old, and have given up on ever intending to marry again, would I experience a truly positive friendship which developed into a real, solid understanding of what it takes to have an equal, respective teamwork-type of a relationship. Any other mismatched relationships were bound to suffer heavy consequences as I found out.

CHAPTER 13

COLLEGE AND CAREER AMBITIONS

All through my senior year in high school, it was my desire to attend a medical college such as the University of Iowa at Iowa City. However, my parents strongly opposed that choice for me. After all, in three previous generations, my mother, grandmother, and great-grandfather had been teachers. My mother insisted that I should follow in their paths, but she told me that if several years down the road I didn't like teaching, I could change to a medical career later. In the first place, there was no money available to assist with my college education, and perhaps the thinking was that since I would need to work myself through college, it would be cheaper to earn a teaching credential than to complete medical school. Reluctantly, I agreed to follow the teaching field, at least temporarily.

Money saved from my very first babysitting jobs, working as a photo coloring artist in a photography studio, a salesperson in the infants section of Sears, detasseling corn for a seed company, and finally raising a bull from a week-old calf until I sold him at an auction for $500 all made my first year of college a reality. Actually, there was enough money to cover a full year and a half of college. The following Monday after I graduated from high school, I left for Cedar Falls. Midway through my first year, my parents insisted that I should return home in order to help my mother who was scheduled for gall bladder surgery. I enrolled at Mason City Junior College during that term and carried a heavy load of twenty-four units while I was helping on the farm caring for my mother and the house. A few of my courses—trigonometry, English, drama, speech, and argumentative debate—took hours of time in homework each night. The drama department presented the play, *One Foot in Heaven*, and I was assigned as assistant director as well as to be Maria. Fortunately I was able to return to Iowa State Teachers College for the spring and summer terms. By the end of that summer, I had enough credits for an emergency teaching credential. I applied for positions which were open, was interviewed, and was immediately hired by the superintendent of Arlington Public School, which was located about 150 miles south and east of my hometown, Mason City. I was nineteen years old at the time of my first teaching position. I managed to arrange for a ride to Arlington, found a room to rent for $40 a month, and with a salary of $180 a month, I was able to eat and still save enough money to pay for another year and a half of college. After three years of teachers college and my student teaching, I was able to receive a Minnesota teaching credential which allowed me to accept a first-grade teaching position in St. Louis Park, Minnesota. I began teaching in September 1953 and married Dale Henry on April 9, 1954. With the exception of one term at the University of Minnesota, I did not return to college until 1962, at which time I finished my bachelor of arts degree at California State University of Los Angeles in 1963, and followed that by earning a master of arts degree, teaching and administrative credentials from the same university in 1968.

Throughout the years, I have followed my interests in medicine and medical research but never had the time or money to make the change in my career. Several times I was able to volunteer alongside a medical team of doctors in Mexico as they provided a free clinic to the people there every month. My knowledge and experiences came in very handy there as we took temperatures and blood pressure and wrote brief descriptions of symptoms and complaints of each patient. Then the prescribed medications were packaged and presented to each patient. Often I was able to perform the whole process with the doctor's approval. The volunteers greatly sped up the process, and I felt a great amount of satisfaction in being able to be of such service. This is a most rewarding experience. There is such a great need for medical assistance throughout the world. I believe that if I could have taken up a medical career that I would have found much success and fulfillment in that field.

CHAPTER 14

SMALL-TOWN VERSUS MIDDLE-TOWN AMERICA

The population of my hometown, Mason City, Iowa, was about thirty-three thousand in the 1940s and 1950s, and it actually remains the same size and number now seventy years later. Even though we lived in town for several years and on different farms in nearby rural areas of Mason City, I still considered all my early life experiences to have been those of a middle-sized Midwestern town. Years later upon moving to the greater Los Angeles area, I found out what it is really like to live in a big city, with freeway gridlock, multicultural communities, crime, and congested living conditions.

Teaching my first year in a little town called Arlington, Iowa, with a population of only six hundred was a totally new experience for me. This was long before I owned a car, so I had to find a ride and move to Arlington, which was about 150 miles from my home. Three teachers in that new school were renting rooms upstairs in an older home on Main Street. When I inquired about renting a room, I found out that the dining room in that same house could be converted into another bedroom and I would need to share the upstairs bathroom with the other teachers. This was a suitable arrangement for me, and I would only need to walk two blocks through the little town's business district and then one more block to reach the only school in town where I would be teaching. There was only one small restaurant in this town, where I ordered the same menu every evening for the whole school year and that being a ground steak, mashed potatoes, and a vegetable for $1.79. After all, I was interested in saving as much money as I possibly could. I often laughed at the sign that hung on the wall above the booth where I sat every day; it read, "Our steaks are so tender that we wonder how the cow ever walked." Their steaks were always excellent, so I ordered the same thing every day.

One day as I was walking to school in the morning, the owner of the local furniture store came out to the sidewalk in front, greeted me with a smile, and invited me to come inside and see his new shipment of coffins which had just arrived. He was so excited and thrilled about his new coffins. I was always suspicious about the underlying intentions of every man I met, but I thanked him, said I didn't have time but might stop in later. As I walked home after school on another day, he again came out in front and again insisted that I come in to see his coffins. I thought this was very strange and unusual; therefore, I suspected either no one has shown an interest in his merchandise, or he had been watching me pass his store every day and was trying to solicit or entice me. I did nervously enter the furniture store, took a quick glance at his room of coffins, told him they were very nice, and left immediately. I always thought that he must have had some sinister plot in his mind and that girls must always be on guard and never get into a position where you could become trapped or seduced. I was greeted many times after that; however, my intuition kept any conversations at bay.

Everyone in town knew everyone by name. I seemed to be the only newcomer in town that year. Not only did everyone know every other person, but they had a way of knowing everything that everyone did. After selecting the First Christian Church to attend, I was asked to direct their choir and to sing solos once in a while. I also sang duets with their minister. He was single and had never married, and I had to be careful so that rumors wouldn't start flying simply because I sang duets with him. One of my required teaching assignments was to be the chaperone and scorekeeper for the boy's high school basketball team, and that meant chaperoning their bus trips and games all over the state of Iowa. That year of 1952, this team won the state championship in basketball. I was still nineteen years old, and most of the football players were seventeen or eighteen. I kept a very professional and mature image in that position. It was enjoyable and fun to see them win and to be responsible for their safety and welfare. On the other hand, there was one senior, who did not go out for sports due to his workload on his father's farm, but who was in instead in the high school drama club. He used to stop into my classroom after drama and just chat. He had a wonderful sense of humor, and I enjoyed visiting with him. By the time my twentieth birthday arrived in May of that year, he began to urge me for a date. I explained that as a teacher I would never be allowed to date a student, and therefore, I could not accept his invitations. After his graduation ceremony, he walked over and gave me a big kiss and said that now that he had graduated from high school, he could date me. Later he did drive probably seventy miles to where I was attending college and made a surprise visit. He said that his intentions were to convince me to quit dating the serviceman, Dale, with whom I had been dating and whom I was corresponding with regularly. He said that he believed that relationship would be entirely wrong for me. He insisted that I should discontinue that relationship and date him instead. I found his personality to be charming but uncomfortably forward and declined his suggestions. Years later, he called me on the phone and said that he had not forgotten me. It was amazing to me that he could track my whereabouts, and I wondered how so many women are vulnerable to be unknowingly searched out, followed, and even preyed upon.

There was a family in the little town of Arlington who had thirteen children. They had so many children that they started giving them away. I taught kindergarten that year, and their son, whom we'll call Anthony, was in my class. He had curly blond hair with big blue eyes and was very unassuming. I worried about whether he would be put up for adoption that year, knowing that at least two other brothers had seemingly been given up for adoption. Another child, whom we'll call Mary, was living with her mother; and the whole town knew about her mother's drinking habits and the many different men in her life. She always came to school looking forlorn, unclean, tattered and listless. I wondered how she would be able to survive in life with such a confusing home life. Erhart, another kindergarten child, was an only child, but he acted as if he were a miniature farmer. He always wore full-length, neatly starched, and freshly ironed pin-striped overalls with metal buckles to school. Usually when he volunteered to go to the front of the class for share time, he would place his hands in his pockets, arch his back, place one foot a little ahead of the other foot, and say things like "Last night when my family was cogitating at the dinner table we discussed the president of the United States and what he was planning for the future of our country." I was amazed by his vocabulary, his formidable stance, and his intelligence. I always wondered if he appeared to stay the same age over his whole lifetime.

Originally, I had been hired by a superintendent who had promised many supplies for the new kindergarten program which I was assigned to create and teach. There had never been a kindergarten class in this town before. It had always been one school with grades one through twelve. It was unfortunate that this superintendent accepted a different job the week after he hired me. When I arrived at the Arlington Public School, there was a completely new superintendent, and his philosophy did not include a kindergarten program for children as young as five years old. He did not want to provide anything more than tables, chairs, paper, pencils, and crayons for this new class. Additionally, the thirty-eight children were required to attend school a full day from 8:00 a.m. until 4:00 p.m. because the bus only makes one scheduled trip throughout the farm areas to pick up children each day. This was really a big challenge for me as a new teacher. I was told that the board wanted every child to learn how to read and write, but they did not supply books or a curriculum. I borrowed supplies from the first-grade teacher, persuaded the superintendent to purchase reading books and workbooks for both reading and math. I also requested some easels, paints, brushes, and building blocks. Then I presented a proposal to the board whereby the kindergarten students could attend school on alternate days. Group 1 would consist of nineteen children who would attend on Monday, Wednesday, and Friday; and group 2 children could attend on Tuesday, Thursday, and Friday. This idea was finally accepted, and it became much easier to teach the students when they were in smaller groups. The year living and teaching in a small rural town was a wonderful experience for me. Having saved enough money for another year and a half of college, I returned to Iowa State Teachers College for the summer term. It was a very busy summer doing student teaching in a third grade in the college elementary campus school. After teaching for one year, student teaching was indeed a pleasure.

During that summer college session, I had a dinner date with Ellis, whom I had met two years prior at that banquet with my mother. He said he could not imagine why I was in a long-distance-correspondence relationship with Dale. He had known him well since they attended college four years together. Now interestingly enough, my mother had handpicked only two men throughout my life that she thought I should marry. One was Ellis, and the other was Dan. Well, Ellis and I had only that one dinner date, and I discovered that he had such an explosive temper that I would not date him again. I never dated Dan, but he later married Betty and had four children with her. After the fourth child was born, he decided to choose an alternate lifestyle; and years later, they divorced.

After the summer term of 1952, I enrolled at Bethel College in St. Paul, Minnesota, where I would be near my family, who had now moved to a forty-acre farm near Buffalo, Minnesota. Upon renting a room in an attic across the street from the college, I carried a full load of classes and took a streetcar to work every day downtown at a dress shop called the Three Sisters. I had to study harder at this college than ever before, but probably it was because in addition to a full schedule, I was required to take a course called the Parallel Gospels of Matthew, Mark, Luke and John and another called the Old Testament, both of which I found to be extremely difficult. I studied several hours every night and into the wee hours. I continued taking voice lessons and even sang a solo in an opera performance. This type of singing seemed very unnatural and difficult. I became much too nervous while singing a solo at a large concert. The course on choir directing was much more enjoyable for me. Somehow I knew that I would need these skills in the future. A traveling gospel-music team was forming, and they requested that I join and be their chalk-drawing artist. There was a large easel facing the audience on which I would draw a complete full-color picture while the other musicians would sing hymns and songs. Before and after my chalk drawing, I would also sing in a trio or a quartet. We traveled on weekends throughout Iowa and Minnesota, giving our presentations at many different churches. At the end of each service, we would present my picture as a gift to someone in the audience. Years later, I was surprised to notice one of my pictures which had been framed and was hanging in a home which I visited.

Three different dates with college or seminary men are indelible in my memory from that term at Bethel. One date was with Wilbur, the same name as that of my father, who was preparing to become a minister in the North Dakota area. He seemed too forward and talked of marriage on our first and only date. The next one, Hal, had spent five years as a prisoner of war in a German prison camp. My one dinner date with him seemed normal enough until we walked past a wooded lot on our way home from the restaurant, where he quickly grabbed and threw me onto the ground and began attacking me. I was so angry that I threatened to notify the college administrators. He actually stopped immediately and continued walking with me to my apartment without another word ever being said. I learned later that he married soon after that and left as a missionary in Japan. The third person I dated, Gary, I had met years prior in Iowa. I would never have remembered him except that he heard that I was attending Bethel, called me, and came there for a lovely dinner date. He was planning to move to the state of Washington and was interested in marriage. It seemed to me that every man I ever dated was up front only interested in marriage. Marriage was something which I hoped would be in my future, but I wanted a solid relationship to develop with a compatible soul mate and one who would be involved in similar types of Christian ministry.

Toward the end of this term at Bethel, I learned that Bethel was not offering any further education courses during the next term which would lead toward a teaching credential. I needed a teaching credential, so I immediately returned to Iowa State Teachers College at Cedar Falls, Iowa, in January in order to complete my associate of arts degree by the end of the following summer. Weeks prior to my graduation in the summer of 1953, I accepted a first-grade teaching position at St. Louis Park, Minnesota. Teaching was something that I really enjoyed, and it was a job where I felt that I could make a difference in the world. When I was handed a check at the end of each month, I always felt surprised that I was being paid for doing something that I enjoyed so much.

CHAPTER 15

RETURNING FROM WAR

Excitement was in the air as soldiers began returning home after the Korean War. The song "When Johnny Comes Marching Home Again" became popular. There was a great amount of anticipation; and everyone looked forward to meeting their sons, husbands, and sweethearts at the gangplank, the airport, bus depot or train stations. Of course, I had expected the same excitement when Dale returned. We had dated about six months prior to his leaving, talked of marriage, and corresponded throughout his eighteen months in Korea. I finally received a brief letter in which he stated that he had arrived back in the States and he would be stationed on the West Coast for several weeks. Surprisingly, I never heard from him again until I made a call and spoke with him. He seemed reserved and rather distant, and I wondered why his demeanor was suddenly different from his letters in which he always hoped to see me soon and longed to be home with me again. I felt that I had quite an emotional stake in our relationship of three years. He had already told me about my engagement ring, for which he had been making monthly payments during his time overseas. Momentarily, I felt confused and disappointed since during our phone conversation he did not make any mention of ever planning to see me again. I anxiously asked when I would be able to see him, but he merely said he would call me after he is discharged from the army.

Correspondence from Dale while he was serving in Korea had become rather sporadic, but I tended to overlook that and accept his welcome and loving letters when they did arrive. Little did I know until many months after his return and our impending marriage that he was seemingly keeping our relationship as a "backup," since I was to find out very soon that he had been living with the clockmaker's daughter as well as having several other Korean girlfriends during the time he was overseas. I would never have found out about that except that his aunt Flora asked me to take his army uniforms to the cleaners. I had been invited to spend Thanksgiving vacation in their home in Dunkerton, Iowa. While making sure that all the pockets were empty before leaving his uniforms at the cleaners, I discovered a full set of pictures taken of him with the clockmaker's daughter in pajamas and in their bedroom. Discovering those pictures suddenly made our relationship seem a sham. I took off the diamond which he had given to me a few months earlier, threw it on the table, told him that our marriage was off. I immediately caught a bus in the middle of a big snowstorm and returned to my teaching position in St. Louis Park near Minneapolis, Minnesota. Dale had entered Grace Seminary in Winona Lake, Indiana, that September of 1953 and had only returned briefly to his home in Dunkerton, Iowa, for our rendezvous during Thanksgiving vacation. Additionally, a bridal shower had been arranged for me that weekend, which happened the evening before our breakup. One lady at the shower had taken me aside and whispered, "You are very brave to be marrying him." After giving her a perplexed look and wondering what she meant, she continued, "Well, you know, you must know." Yes, I was aware that he often said things that seemed unusual and out of the ordinary, but people seemed to accept his manner of speaking as if he somehow had a unique Southern sense of humor and almost a hint of a Southern drawl. He was, after all, a college graduate, "tall, dark, and handsome," as they say. He had prayed to God when he was wounded on his second day on the front lines in Korea, promising God that he would serve Him for the rest of his life if only God would keep him alive. That was the main reason why he said that he enrolled in seminary and decided to become a minister, or possibly it was because the GI Bill would pay him $160 a month to continue his education. He was intellectually inclined toward anything to do with history. Bible history definitely fit into his love and uncanny understanding of historical events. He seemed to remember and identify with history in a way as if he had been there and knew all about it. He never forgot anything that he ever learned about history. I had been fully trained and qualified to administer the Stanford-Binet intelligence quotient test, so I asked him to and let me practice giving the test and administer it to him. He was brilliant, just as I thought, with an intelligence quotient of over 145. What could that lady have been talking about at my shower that continued to haunt my mind? Even so, the day I found those pictures, I emotionally retreated as anger and doubts flooded my mind and overshadowed our relationship.

The teachers at Elliot School, where I was teaching in St. Louis Park, immediately noticed that I was no longer wearing my engagement ring. A surge of freedom overwhelmed my emotions as if I had been relieved of a burden that just seemed too heavy to bear. Obviously, my relationship had not been working out for me. Hadn't both of my parents warned me about this relationship? We had recently met and visited for a week at my parents' home on their farm in Buffalo, Minnesota. He spent some of his time helping my father with chores while I continued driving back and forth to my teaching position. He seemed to have only one thing on his mind, and that was that I should become as sexually involved with him as I later learned that he had become accustomed to when he was overseas. I refused to compromise my standards.

My parents took me aside after his visit, and with great emotion, they each tried to convince me that he was not a person that I should ever marry. My father said that when he helped him with chores in the barn, he expressed anger, yelling and swearing at the cows, often embarrassing my father. This was very hard for me to accept, and I mentally denied that it could be possible. My parents continued by urging me to discontinue my plans for marriage. They worried as to how he might treat children in a marriage. I thought they were just against anyone whom I would date. Later, of course, I remembered those warnings after I broke off our engagement.

I soon became interested in another friend who seemed very professional and kind. We became friends but never dated as I hoped we would because no sooner had Christmas come and gone than Dale began calling me from Indiana, where he was attending seminary, begging forgiveness, crying over and over again on the phone and saying that he wanted to quit the seminary and transfer to Northwestern Seminary in Minneapolis to be near me. This did not seem like a good idea to me, but his calls continued almost daily until I began to reason that I should not stop him from transferring to Northwestern if he really wanted to attend that school. I gave no assurance that I would ever date him again. He did the most incredible thing that I could ever imagine; he quit Grace Seminary and moved into the men's dormitory on the second floor above the preschool which my parents owned in Minneapolis. This became a very awkward situation for me. He began working part-time as an assistant in my parent's preschool. When he wasn't in seminary, working, or living with my parents, he would be hanging out in my apartment, which was located in the apartment building right next door to Northwestern University, where he enrolled and began attending. It seemed as if his life depended upon marrying me. He threatened that if I would not marry him immediately, he would go out on the street and marry the next lady in a skirt that he met. That should have been the biggest red flag of all to me; however, somehow the intensity of this threat made me feel sorry for him. I told him that I would let him know later. I wrestled with my conscience. My reasoning was as follows: 1) He had promised to serve God for the rest of his life and as a Christian this was honorable and important to me; 2) He was already living with and working for my family. Therefore, he had already become included in my family; 3) He was tall, good-looking, and intelligent; 4) His mother died when he was four years old and he probably had a difficult life; 5) He had the potential, I believed, to become a good husband; 6) He had picked out my engagement ring before he left for Korea and made payments every month while serving in Korea, which showed clear intentions (in spite of his many escapades over there); 7) I considered myself as very capable, and I would be able to accept this as a calling from God to be his wife and serve with him in ministry for my whole life; 8) I knew that I could be supportive, and with God's help, everything could work out for the best. I made my decision by the end of the week, agreed to let bygones be bygones, and would be willing to marry him late in the summer. I still had reservations and wanted more time to be sure. He insisted, and won, to have our marriage take place during Easter vacation, which was only three weeks away.

The teachers at my school were in a total uproar about my announcement. They said that it was obvious that I must be pregnant; otherwise, I never would have agreed to marry him so quickly. They would not listen to any other reason. He had only met the teachers in my school one time when he came for lunch. At that time, I had become embarrassed when he seemed to appear too friendly with my principal, who was Catholic and very prudish; however, in turn she showed that she was more than a little fond of his attention.

Our courtship period had consisted of one miniature-golf game, attending church together, seeing one travelogue at college, visiting at each other's homes and a lot of correspondence which spanned three and a half years. Activities which I loved such as ice skating, skiing, hiking, camping, singing, playing the piano, and working hard were activities which literally disgusted him. He always made condescending remarks concerning any of these activities. Common interests, however, which we shared, included studying the Bible, going for rides in the country, listening to music, visiting and entertaining our many friends. He was an excellent teller of jokes, and he told his favorite lengthy jokes over and over everywhere we went. He liked to eat, but not to cook. There was only one time in my recollection in which he offered to cook, and that was on our first dinner date at his apartment in college. That was memorable because he accidentally used powdered detergent from a jar above the stove in place of flour when making gravy. After the gravy foamed and flowed all over the stove, he realized his mistake. This provided many laughs for his roommate, Bill Shaw, who was an excellent cook.

My advice to couples contemplating marriage is to first seek God's will and wisdom and secondly to pay attention to all the subtle red flags which may or may not seem important at the time. Marriage needs to be considered more like a business partnership with equal investment of time, energy, enthusiasm, commitment, interests, and especially spiritual attunement. Additionally, friends and family who are not as close to the decision-making process can also provide important clues as to how they see your relationship. Hindsight is a great teacher. Of course, I not only had the question marks, clues from family and friends; but I also neglected to rely more heavily on the great wisdom of God. When threatened, pushed, intimidated, or coerced, I should have called for help. Thinking that I was strong enough to overcome any obstacles was a grave error to make on my part.

It would be my earnest prayer that anyone who has any doubts at all should lean toward ending the relationship and waiting for a more compatible relationship. A lifetime is a long time to live in a situation that is not compatible or working smoothly for both partners. Divorce is worse than death and should be avoided if at all humanly possible.

Marriage: Rev. Dale Henry, Phyllis,
Curtis 5, Cathy 3½, David 10 months

CHAPTER 16

GETTING MARRIED

T he wedding was beautiful, and the church was full. Rev. Meyers, a close friend of my parents from their Bible college days in St. Paul, Minnesota, officiated at the wedding. The students from my first-grade class, along with their parents, filled the balcony. Friends and relatives arrived from near and far. The gifts were extraordinarily lovely. The gorgeous wedding gown that I wore made me feel special. Dale certainly was a tall, dark, and handsome groom. I was now reconciled to my decision, my commitment, and my new job as a loyal, supportive wife forever and until death would we part.

We rented a very, very small studio apartment with a Murphy bed on the second floor in an apartment building about two blocks away from my former apartment. This apartment as well as my former apartment both overlooked beautiful Loring Park, so we felt that the view made up for the small size. Dale continued in seminary for the next two and a half years, and I continued teaching the following year after our marriage. One of my greatest desires in life was to have children. Remembering that Dr. Eggloff told me when I was thirteen that I probably would never be able to have children due to having rheumatic fever twice as a child, I hoped and prayed that I could have a child. I was healthy, active, and had never had any physical or health problems throughout my teenage years. Now I was twenty-one, had completed three years of college, and had taught school for two years; surely I was healthy enough to have a child. I wanted to have a baby more than anything else. Ten months passed, and I seemed unable to become pregnant, which caused me to begin to be extremely worried and concerned. I remembered that Dale had already told me when we were dating that there were two things in life that he hated; one was travelogues, and the other was children. I always knew that he really did not want children, but I hoped that he might change his mind. Finally, in late February of 1955, I learned that I was pregnant. I had mentioned to one of my teacher friends earlier that I was hoping to have a baby. No sooner than that rumor got around than I was called into the principal's office in mid-February of 1955. She said, "I see that you are pregnant, with your round tummy, and you know that no one is allowed to teach in this district when they are pregnant. Therefore, you will need to leave your teaching job immediately." This was more than a shock to me. I was less than one month pregnant, so someone must have told her of my intentions. I certainly did not have a round tummy; I still weighed 110 pounds, the same weight as the day I got married; I never had morning sickness; and I could not believe her spiteful attitude. I wanted to think positively, so I resigned and enrolled the next week for the spring quarter at the University of Minnesota. This was a very rewarding term and would be valuable to me in the future because it was there that I learned how to do research for my own research projects in the future.

I was never sick a single day during my pregnancy. In fact, I felt empowered and healthier than I had ever felt in my life. I was active in sports, hiking, and even pedaling a paddlewheel boat a few miles across a lake two days before giving birth. Dale was an excellent softball player. He was known for hitting the balls farther than anyone else could on the teams for which he played. He played on different church and local teams, and I rarely missed sitting in the bleachers, watching with amazement as he hit the ball hundreds of yards allowing him to make many home runs.

My income from teaching had been good, and I still had a small nest egg left in my savings; but now that I was not working, we needed to live on $160 a month which was still being provided by his GI Bill. This monthly allotment would be increased $20 a month after our baby was born, but that would still not be enough for us to live on. Dale had taken an evening job as a clerk at a small hotel, but that job lasted only a few months. He had fallen asleep on the job and his position was terminated that same night. Then we really had to improvise and live on our most meager income.

Baby Curtis Dean was born on September 16, 1955. Our troubles were just beginning to surface. Dale seemed extremely jealous of any attention which I gave to our baby. It became difficult to nurse the baby, cook, clean, type Dale's assignments, assist him with memorizing his sermons, help him memorize Greek and Hebrew vocabulary, and also keep up our busy social life.

When Curtis was four months old, we had scheduled to have him dedicated, similar to a baby baptismal service at the church where our longtime minister friend, Rev. Terry Hulbert, was preaching. We were dressed, in the car driving to the church, when Dale abruptly stated that he was not going to allow his child to be dedicated. He was so angry that he laid rubber with the car, turned it around, and said that he would not go to church that day. I was in total disbelief. It was the first angry outburst which I had ever seen from him. I remember quietly rationalizing to myself that Dale himself was preparing to be a minister. Rev. Terry Hulbert was expecting our baby to be dedicated, and our friends and family would be there also. Dale was so angry that we couldn't even discuss the matter further. We did not attend church that Sunday, and I was left to make reasonable excuses or explanations to Rev. Terry Hulbert, my parents, and our friends. It also came into my mind that he might be having another symptom or reaction to his near fatal injuries on the front lines during the Korean War. I had seen another similar reaction from him just prior to this episode where he abruptly laid on the ground during a "fly over" at a nearby air show. Was this another explosive reaction from his war experiences I wondered? There seems to be a better understanding these days about the post traumatic war syndrome, even though little seems to be done to rehabilitate our returning soldiers.

A few weeks later, Curtis contracted a severe viral strain of influenza from which many babies died that winter in the Minneapolis area. Fortunately, I had kept my Blue Cross family health insurance plan in force, so this did not present a financial crisis in addition to the emotional and physical strain on all of us. During his hospitalization, it became necessary to hire a nurse to stay with him around-the-clock for at least two days while he was being given IV through the vein in his heel. He had become severely dehydrated, but he did respond to the treatment. He suffered with diarrhea for three months after that illness. Finally, the doctors, as a last resort, required that he drink only tea for several days, which finally cleared up his intestinal problems. Without funds to continue renting an apartment for our family, we arranged to live in my parents' vacant farmhouse near Buffalo, Minnesota. The farmhouse lacked indoor bathroom facilities, and I had to walk nearly a quarter of a mile in the snow in order to wash diapers in the river. That was really tough.

Already, we were on such a tight budget that we were not able to purchase things we felt we needed unless it was the barest essential. That was the reason we had to give up our apartment and move temporarily out to the empty farmhouse. Times were very difficult, and with a new baby, there was no way that I could work. Dale graduated in the spring of 1955 with a bachelor of divinity and said that he wanted to continue attending college to pursue yet another degree. He still had at least one more year on the GI Bill left, and somehow he reasoned that we could live on $180 per month from his GI Bill. By this time, I was beginning to get discouraged. It seemed to me that Dale's greatest interest in life was to become a perpetual student. I had already helped support our little family financially, typed his term papers, and helped him with many of his assignments. I expressed my feelings that I felt that it was necessary for him to get a job in order to support our family.

I was just beginning to realize that Dale really did not seem to want to get a job. I suggested that he apply for a Minnesota teaching credential and teach there in the fall. He did not want to do that under any circumstance. So we moved our little family into one room in the boys' dorm which my parents owned. I pleaded with him to get a job. Instead, and unbeknownst to me, he called the former minister of the church in Waterloo, Iowa, where he and Dan had attended during college and asked if he knew of any job opening in California. As a matter of fact, Rev. Hohenstein said the Christian school which was located next door to the Brethren Church in Whittier, California, where he was the pastor, was looking for a sixth-grade teacher. The salary of $260 a month was small, but he knew of a furnished apartment in a house for $65 a month, which would be adequate for us if he decided to accept this position. Dale was excited about the possibility of this offer, and he began making arrangements to move to California. He acted as if he would go there alone, but he wanted me to decide if I would go with him. This was another time in which I would need to make another big decision in my life. Should I stay in Minnesota with my parents and not go to California with the many unknowns out there? Again I had to follow a pattern of reasoning: 1) Since Dale seemed so negatively influenced and frequently upset by his aunt and uncle, who had been his foster parents since he was four, maybe he needed to move farther away from them; and 2) since he would at least be taking a job and starting to receive an income; and 3) since we had no place to live except for this one room in my parents' boys' dormitory; and 4) since I had just found out that I was two and a half months pregnant with a second child; and finally 5) since I really did want our marriage to succeed, I would therefore agree to move to California. I had never been that far away from home, and I really did not know what to expect on such a long trip.

We had no time to waste and would need to leave within two or three days. Everything we owned was packed into or on top of the 1952 Plymouth coupé that Dale had purchased after he got out of the army. We packed the ironing board, the baby crib, my sewing machine and cabinet (dismantled) our silverware, dishes, clothes, sheets, blankets, and some food for the trip. I can still picture in my mind this little car, packed at least four feet high on top. It was loaded. Certainly, after eighteen months of marriage, we should be able to make a clean start and live happily ever after.

The trip was long and tedious. It was late August, and the weather was hot and dry as we traveled through the desert. The car was so heavily packed that there was only about a two-foot crawl space in the backseat area for Curtis to sleep. We did not have air-conditioning in the car; therefore using water and damp cloths was the only way to try to keep cool. It was a long time to sit in the car, being pregnant and uncomfortable.

We had hopes of a new beginning with new friends and a new little home for our family. We seemingly had no fears of upcoming homesickness, financial problems, or even problems with the car. We were naive to say the least, and *naive* was hardly the best word for it.

Little did I know that another eight years would bring about the total destruction of our marriage as well as that of our growing family.

CHAPTER 17

CHILDREN ARE GIFTS FROM HEAVEN

Curtis had his first birthday the week after we arrived in California. He was a beautiful child and had such a delightful, bubbly personality. I had hoped it would be different, but it really didn't matter a whole lot to me that he received almost no attention from his father. I was at home with him all the time; and I would try my best to train him to be wise, loving, resourceful, and helpful. He had begun walking at nine months of age and toilet-trained himself at the same time. He would not allow himself to have an accident. By the time he was one year old, he began to gain the weight he had lost during his long illness, and he soon became a totally healthy child. He loved the outdoors, the sunshine, and the neighbor's kitten. The warm California sunshine really agreed with him. At the time of his first birthday, I was three months pregnant. Now Dale had been very explicit in stating that he did not want another child, but I believed that there should be either two or four children in a family. An only child often has a difficult time without any siblings, and three was always an awkward number. I should know because there were three children in my family. In order to at least have two children, I planned ahead to become pregnant at the exact date when I could conceive. All went well, and a second child was conceived exactly on schedule. It had been confirmed by my doctor that I was expecting prior to leaving Minnesota on that long trip to California. The temperature had reached 121 degrees the day in September when we reached Needles, California. We had no air-conditioning in our car and no seat belts; and Curtis, who was trying to sleep on the bed we had arranged on top of all the packed items in the backseat, was flushed and gasping from the heat. I had been sponging him with water for several hours until we decided to stop at a motel in Needles, rent a room for a couple of hours during the heat of the day, and then spend an hour or two swimming in the pool. This stop really refreshed us, and we set out again in the early evening. I said that we were going east and in the wrong direction on the highway, and Dale argued that we were driving west. He finally saw signs indicating that we were indeed traveling back the way we had come. He drove a long way to the next off-ramp, turned around, and began driving west and up the long steep incline ahead. There were several automobiles alongside the highway where their radiators had boiled over. Some cars had heavy canvas bags of water hanging out in front of the hood so that the evaporation of the water would help keep the radiator cool as well as provide extra water in case it was needed.

It seemed a miracle that we didn't have any car trouble. I was very concerned about having car trouble since Dale by his own admission was not mechanically inclined, and any problems with the car would have been a disaster, especially in the heat. We finally arrived in Whittier; and it looked like paradise with palm trees, green grass, flowers everywhere, and a huge fountain in the middle of the circular roadway when we entered Whittier from Beverly Boulevard on the north side. The little front apartment of the house which was reserved for us to rent was clean and furnished. Everything seemed perfect, except for the fact that we couldn't live on the salary which Dale was to receive and I was pregnant and probably could not get a job.

I decided that I must get a job anyway if we were to eat, and I soon arranged to teach kindergarten in the mornings and music for grades one through six during the afternoon sessions at the Norwalk Brethren School in Norwalk. This meant sharing our one car; dropping Dale off at his job in Whittier; taking Curtis to a babysitter and then driving about twenty miles to teach all day in Norwalk and then returning to pick up Curtis and then Dale; cook, clean, care for Curtis; and begin to plan for the arrival of another new baby in late March. I was extremely concerned about telling the principal at this school about my pregnancy after my experience in St. Louis Park, and I made sure that I didn't show that I was expecting until at least February.

They did not have any other teacher to take my place, so when I told them that I was expecting, they reluctantly agreed to let me teach until the week before our Catherine Rose was born on March 29, 1957.

Cathy, as we nicknamed her, was the most beautiful baby I had ever seen. She was born at the City of Angels Medical Center, a Presbyterian hospital in Los Angeles. Dr. Kroener Jr., my obstetrician, arranged for me to go there because of a new program whereby babies were allowed to be in the same room with their mother from the moment of birth instead of being placed in a nursery. Unfortunately, when babies were in their mother's room, photographers were not allowed to enter and take pictures; and I really wanted a picture of her, which I never got. She had come into this world very quickly in that we barely had time to arrive at the hospital, sign in, and she was here within the next fifteen minutes. I had signed papers that I wanted to have a natural childbirth without an epidural for the anesthetic. However, the pain was more than I could ever withstand, and I begged for an epidural anyway. The injection had scarcely started to take effect when she was born. The ride to the hospital was also traumatic. I woke Dale up at about 11:15 p.m., begging and insisting that I had to be taken to the hospital immediately if not sooner. I just knew the time was short. He drove very slowly on purpose because he argued that when Curtis was born, he drove nearly ninety miles an hour, but the baby was not born for yet another eighteen hours; therefore he knew he could drive forty miles an hour on the freeway and still have plenty of time. I almost lost my patience. Sometimes, nothing would change his mind. Dale had received an extension of one year in order to complete his final thesis for Northwestern Seminary. I had been typing frantically in my spare time, and I was on page 179 the night Cathy was born. There were still about sixty-five pages for me to finish typing after I got home from the hospital. There was no time to waste, or he would miss his deadline for turning in his thesis whereby the seminary would honor his BS degree in theology.

*   *   *

Children are definitely gifts from heaven, and bringing children into the world is probably the greatest thrill that any woman will ever experience. My whole career was centered on how to train, care for, and educate children. I considered my children as my first priority and highest calling in life. I knew that I wanted children and was always sorry that their father could not recognize them as the greatest treasures on earth until much, much later in his life. Our children would never be able to have me at home as a full-time mother, but they still were my first priority, and I determined that every minute that I would have with them would be of the highest quality that I was humanly able to give them.

Smog was a big problem in those days. I had been driving back and forth for more than six weeks from Whittier to Norwalk when I first saw the mountain range to the north. I was so surprised. I took Curtis for a short ride on the north side of the Whittier hills, where there was a large dairy farm. He loved to see the cows up close and watch them eat hay. While we were there, he looked up and saw Mount Baldy, which was completely covered with snow. He pointed and shrieked, "Big ice-cream cone!" Now that he mentioned it, I laughed and did notice the resemblance.

Someone in the Whittier Brethren Church loaned us a baby dresser for Cathy after she was born. She had the baby clothes left over from Curtis but did not have a dress or anything new for her until she was three weeks old and there was no baby shower. My mother finally sent a lovely white nylon dress for her. It was very pretty, and we received it just in time for the upcoming baby dedication which had been announced at church. Now for some reason, Dale insisted on both children being dedicated at the Whittier Brethren Church. I was surprised beyond belief. I had not forgotten the outrage which he had displayed in Minneapolis when Curtis was scheduled to be dedicated. I wondered why there was such a change of heart. Could it be that his image in the community was more important to him now? Would he go through with it this time, or would he refuse at the last minute? Curtis was now nearly two years old and Cathy was three months and it seemed a little late for Curtis to be involved in a baby dedication service. At any rate, all went well, and we had a family picture taken after the service.

At the completion of Dale's teaching contract that spring, the board decided they would not renew his contract for the following year, and he would be without a job again. What would happen next? Would he be able to find a job? Would I be able to work with two babies? What is the plan that God has for us now? I wondered.

CHAPTER 18

JOB DESCRIPTION FOR A MINISTER'S WIFE

D ale applied for a minister position in a fairly new Brethren Church in Temple City, California, which had a small congregation and a Christian school of about one hundred students. He preached there one Sunday morning; and the board voted to accept him based on that one sermon, his bachelor's degree in divinity, his teaching credential for Iowa, and the recommendation provided by Rev. Hohenstein of the Brethren Church of Whittier. They would be willing to pay a salary of $300 per month, and we would need to rent the large rambling house next door to the church for $150 a month. Additionally, the minister was expected to tithe ten percent or $30 or more each month. This left approximately $120 for living expenses. The utilities in the big house were about $40 a month, gas and auto expenses for his visits to the parishioners would come to another $30, auto insurance another $20 per month. This left a possible $20 per month for food, medical expenses, and clothing. I suggested that Dale should try to take an additional part-time job, but he wanted to spend all his time serving the church and administering the school as expected by the church board. I personally knew other ministers who had taken on additional part-time jobs in order to supplement their income and to support their families, but he would not even consider that as a possibility. In the meantime, while Dale was attending a church conference in another state, I was required to accompany the church youth group to an outing at a carnival. I was injured when one of the rides malfunctioned and jerked severely during the ride. It turned out that I suffered a whiplash of the neck and was in severe pain for several months. I began taking pain medication and sought relief with chiropractic treatments which we could not afford.

There were many jobs which I was expected to perform "free gratis" as the minister's wife. One of the jobs was to arrange the order of the service, choose the hymns, type the bulletin, and make copies on the old "purple passion" self-cranking mimeograph machine which was available at the church office. Additionally, I was expected to receive phone calls, coordinate workdays for the congregation, play the piano, assist with the supervision of the church school, and be socially involved with the church families. Other jobs such as playing the piano and singing at the missions on skid row in downtown Los Angeles were often required. Those experiences were eye-openers to me. Each and every face seemed to display expressions of rejection, broken heartedness, and failure. Nights when I could not accompany Dale to those services, he would arbitrarily decide to bring a couple of those disheartened men home with him to live in our home. He said that he felt sorry for them and wanted to give them a chance for a better life.

We had personally been surviving on oatmeal, macaroni and cheese, and occasionally a few hot dogs; so how could we feed these homeless men also? I asked. I prepared homemade soup for them and requested that they sweep the driveway and do some work prior to receiving their soup. Well, that angered them; but before I knew it, there were other homeless men arriving at our door. I learned later that one of the men had written a message under the bridge a few miles away, giving directions to the church and our house next door so that they could also receive a "handout." One day, a man who arrived had a story about being out of gas and needing to have a check cashed so he could continue his trip. I was skeptical of him, but Dale seemed to trust his story completely; and when we didn't have very much money in our bank account or extra money to buy food or clothes for ourselves, he went ahead and cashed a check for $25 for that man. The next day, another man met Dale at the church with a similar story. Again, Dale cashed another check for $50. When I found out that Dale had cashed two checks, I told him I was sure that the checks were not good and that they would overdraw our account. He disagreed and insisted that the men were sincere. Well, both checks bounced, and we were overdrawn by $75. The following night, I was awakened as one of the men who was now living in our home got up at about 2:00 a.m. and walked through our baby's bedroom and slipped quietly out the front door. I became alarmed, got up and checked everything, went back to bed, but never went back to sleep. Soon I heard police cars and policemen in the driveway which we shared with the house next door. The police were searching through the garages behind our house and causing quite a commotion, and I noticed that the homeless man who was staying in our home was handcuffed and put in the back seat of the police car. I never did know what the police found, but I suspected that drugs were being stored or hidden in the garages and the drug dealers were picking them up and trading them there. I was literally frightened beyond description. When Dale awoke, I told him that I had been suspicious all along of the homeless men that he was bringing home. I begged him not to bring anyone else to our home or to cash checks for strangers in the future. Fortunately, he agreed, and the homeless men were asked to leave. The other strangers must also have been given the message under the bridge because they stopped coming to our door, begging for food and money.

After about six months living in the big house next to the church, we were able to find a smaller and cheaper house several blocks away from the church, which rented for only $95 a month. It was much quieter in this neighborhood. My grandmother Bauer, who was eighty-five, came from Iowa and stayed with us for a week. She was helpful, peeling potatoes, baking cookies, sweeping the floor, and tidying the house. I talked with her about how difficult things were, and I asked how she had gone through hard times and was now healthy and living into her late eighties. She told me that when she was my age, she didn't think she would make it to her thirties; but taking one day at a time she was able to live a good and long life. I said that I felt the same way because there were so many demands on me from my children, my duties as a minister's wife, and being so very poor. I told her that I sometimes felt like crying when people in our church were able to eat at restaurants on Sunday after church, travel and go on vacations, and we were having such a struggle to merely put food on our table. I told her we had never once been invited out for a meal or to any restaurant, nor had anyone in the church ever given us any food. It was obvious that we were unable to live on so little money. She became sad and told me that I should be able to spend more time at home with the children rather than having to attend all the church services and keep up with the many church activities. Usually, the children attended the services with me. My grandmother stayed home with Curtis and Cathy the next Sunday evening while I attended the service without the children. When I returned, the children were crying and so was my grandmother. She told me the children cried while I was gone and that made her cry also. She was sad and said that I needed to stay home with the children. I felt that she was overly sensitive and that they probably cried because they wanted to go with me. I thanked her and promised her that I would try to limit my activities at the church as much as possible.

From the day we had married, I had been in charge of handling the finances. Somehow, Dale seemed unconcerned as to the amount of money that went into the bank and how that related to the money that was needed to support the family. I tried to cut every corner, but it had become impossible to make ends meet. Once again, I tried unsuccessfully to persuade him to take an additional part-time job. The church was so small that it only needed a part-time minister in the first place; but on his own, he wanted to spend ten to twelve hours a day and seven days a week at his church office, studying, preparing for his sermons, or making house calls on the parishioners. Curtis and Cathy hardly knew who he was. He left in the morning before they woke up, and he never returned until after they had gone to bed. They really only knew him as the preacher who was standing up in front of the church. It was at my insistence that Dale either seek an additional part-time job or request a raise. He chose the latter and finally went before the board on a Wednesday evening and requested a $25-a-month raise. He returned home that night and told me that the board members had refused even a one-dollar raise, and they also told him that they were planning to terminate his employment at the end of the month anyway. We were there approximately one year.

After being dismissed from the church in Temple City, Dale arranged to become the assistant minister to Rev. Hohenstein at the church we had first attended when we moved in California. His assignment was to preach and work with the board in building a new Brethren Church in the city of La Habra, which was about twelve miles away. I suggested that Dale apply for a GI loan in order to purchase a house in Whittier. The house which we purchased was on Wellsford Street, had good neighbors, was small but very nice with a lovely rose garden and a huge walnut tree in the backyard. We were able to purchase it for $11,250, no down payment, low interest, and monthly payments which would be lower than rent. Curtis was turning five and would be going by bus to a public school in Whittier. Shockingly, a third baby was also on the way. It seemed that we had used every form of birth control known at that time. I didn't even recognize that my symptom of constant throbbing in the solar plexus and being extremely tired were indicating another pregnancy. I had no other indication and could not even believe it when my doctor said that I had good reason for my symptoms because he said that I was already over three months pregnant. I could hardly accept this truth. I was caught off guard and had a hard time realizing that a baby was already on the way. Dale, on the other hand, suddenly had a hilarious reaction. He laughed and laughed because he considered this pregnancy to be a joke on me. Since I was already scheduled to teach daily vacation Bible club at the church in Whittier, I would have to decline that job as well as many others. Throughout that whole pregnancy, I never had morning sickness as I had never had it with either of my former two pregnancies. However, I suffered constant pains and throbbing in the solar plexus and diaphragm area. I worried about what the pain meant and prayed constantly, as with each other pregnancy, that my baby would be healthy and normal.

Dale's position as a minister for a new church in La Habra, which was being started in an old remodeled house with a small area to be used as an auditorium, was beginning to falter. Members of the board began questioning me about the fact that they were noticing Dale frequently rolling his eyes upward as if looking up at the ceiling during his sermons almost as if he were having a seizure, they told me. They wondered if he was nervous because I was in the audience. I explained that I was noticing the same thing but that he said he always felt more comfortable when I was in the audience. I spoke to Dale about their concerns, and he denied looking up at the ceiling and said that he was unaware of any such gestures or expressions. However, the actions continued and even increased in frequency. But after another month, the board voted to terminate his employment. Many years later, Dale suffered from a brain tumor, which ruptured prior to a scheduled brain surgery. This in hindsight may have been the first symptom of the condition which the board members complained about. At the time, however, this meant another move again. I stayed behind in Whittier until I sold our little house where we had lived for slightly more than a year for $13,800. Since I sold the house myself to a private party, there was no real estate commission involved, and the closing costs were less than $150. The profit of nearly $2,500 was really needed to pay our debts and give us a little financial boost. Additionally, Dale's grandmother passed away that year at the age of ninety-five, and he was surprised to receive $1,100, which was left to him in her will. He wanted to and did spend all that money on a series of Bible reference books for his library.

Meanwhile, David Russell was born on February 2, 1960. Even though he was a complete surprise, he was most lovable, with a very outgoing personality for a baby. We were so proud of him. Since Dale had thought that his birth was such a joke on me, he extended himself to spend more time enjoying this baby than he had with both of the other children put together. David's birth had been traumatic because the Whittier Presbyterian Hospital, which was newly built and had only opened the day before, was not yet staffed with a doctor. The law, as I found out, would not allow a nurse to deliver a baby without a doctor being present, so two nurses held the baby back by force in the birth canal while both of them yelled and even swore at me to stop pushing until the doctor could arrive. I finally passed out. Dr. William Kroener Jr., who had also delivered our Catherine in 1957, had checked me at 8:30 p.m. that evening and said that I would not deliver until the next day and he would see me in the morning. It was raining heavily when we drove the five blocks to the hospital, and I just knew that I was having the baby that night. I was furious that he left me and that he didn't return in time. The baby was ready to be born at 11:50 p.m. on February 1, 1960, but the nurses were not able to reach the doctor by phone until 12:15 a.m., at which time he said he would go immediately. He arrived at 12:30 a.m. and delivered the baby within the next five minutes. David's neck seemed injured from being held back, and he had difficulty holding his head up until he was nearly nine months old. When he was older, he wanted to sue that doctor for negligently causing his early neck injury which actually bothered him well into adulthood.

I was sorry to move away from the city of Whittier, but Dale accepted a part-time minister position at an Independent Brethren Church near the mountains in Glendora. After accepting the part-time ministering job at the Independent Brethren Church in Glendora, he arranged to rent a very old farmhouse with screened porches on two sides. It was surrounded by fifteen acres of orange groves which were located on Leodora Street in Glendora.

The Independent Brethren Church was very orthodox in its religious doctrine and customs. It was not related in any way to the former Brethren churches where Dale had served. The women in this church kept their heads covered at all times. They wore hand-knitted caps or little white starched cotton bonnets similar to the ones the Pilgrims wore. They also dressed in long, old-fashioned floor-length dresses. They welcomed us and were very friendly and cordial. They were the first people, in this, our third pastorate, who invited us into their homes for meals. The average age of the congregation was approximately seventy to seventy-five with many members in their late eighties and early nineties. Now as a twenty-seven-year-old minister's wife, I found switching to their style of dresses and bonnets an impossible requirement. They would simply have to accept me as I was, I thought, and this certainly did not earn me any brownie points. But since this was only a part-time ministering position, they seemed willing to overlook my more modern knee-length dresses, but I knew that not keeping my head covered was a problem for them. However, to my surprise, they invited me to speak at one of their evening services; and the church was full whereas there had been only a few each Sunday night when Dale was preaching. The people almost seemed to sit on the edge of their seats in order to take in every word I said. Now I had been playing the piano for their services for several months, but that was different than actually telling them what I believed. The congregation seemed more readily able to accept me after I had that opportunity to speak to them from the pulpit.

Chaplains were becoming recognized at that time by the medical profession as being beneficial to patients who spend long hours and days in the hospital. Dale enrolled in a chaplain-training program under the direction of Chaplain Harris at Long Beach Community Hospital. This program was at least forty-five miles away from our home in Glendora and long before the 605 Freeway was built. That meant that he would split his week, stay four nights a week in the home of his cousin Dan in Long Beach, and then come home with us for three days and nights so he could preach at the Independent Brethren Church on Sunday, where his salary for part-time was $200 a month. The chaplain-training program required trainees to solicit donations in order to raise their own support. We found it next to impossible to interest people in donating to this program and specifically to his ministry. We wrote to family, friends, and church members but never raised more than approximately $15 a month or $150 that year, which was then in addition to his other part-time salary. That meant that we would have to budget and live on less than $215 per month. That amount was not sufficient to pay rent, utilities, and gas, leaving nothing for food and clothing.

Spending many nights alone with the children in this old house in the middle of the orange grove was a little scary. There were several nights when I heard all kinds of noises outside of our screened in porches. I even began to suspect that the elderly man who lived about a half a mile down the road might be a peeping Tom. Finally, in desperation, I borrowed a shotgun from a gun collector we had known in Whittier and I kept it under my bed. I remembered how to shoot a gun from the times when I went hunting with my father. To my surprise, when Dale returned on the weekend, he was scared to death of that gun. He did not want a gun anywhere in the house. I told him that he would be perfectly safe if he would just let me know what time he was coming home. Finally, I had to remove the gun and place it on the top shelf at the very back of the closet while he was at home on weekends and then retrieve the gun again after he drove away to return to his chaplaincy training program in Long Beach.

We were going backward financially so fast that I would need to begin working again in order to make ends meet. By this time the only clothing our children received was given to them. It was embarrassing for me. The year prior, my parents had sold their preschool and boys' dormitory business and property in Minneapolis and moved to Whittier, California, in order to be near our children, who were their only grandchildren at that time. While in this desperate financial situation, I asked them if I could borrow some money but was told that I had made my bed and I should lie in it. This began an emotional chasm between me and my parents. How could they not understand that we were without food? I'm sure they sensed our dilemma but wanted to see us solve our problems by ourselves. I rented a small furnished one-room apartment which backed up to the railroad tracks in Long Beach for an additional $40 a month and agreed to teach and help my parents in supervising the elementary division of the private school which they had purchased in August of 1960. They said they would pay me well if I would manage the elementary division and teach the first-grade class full-time also. That meant transferring Curtis from the Glendora first grade into the first grade which I would be teaching. Cathy would enter kindergarten, and David had to be placed in an infant care center. He was eight months old then. At the end of the first pay period, my father presented my first check to me. My check indicated that I was paid the bare minimum hourly wage. I was totally disappointed but reluctantly continued working there until late in November, at which time I contracted the Asian flu. It was the week of Thanksgiving and the teachers were off on vacation for four days. The virus struck me very hard. I canceled the rental of the small apartment and moved full-time into our house in Glendora, where we had been spending our weekends anyway. It took almost three months to recover from that illness.

Toward the spring of that year, the board of the Independent Church of the Brethren in Glendora gave notice to Dale that they were terminating his position. Prior to losing his previous job, I had entered into an agreement with Dale, whereby if he were to lose another ministerial job, he would promise to get out of the preaching ministry and return to teaching or else enter a different career. He had agreed. However, when this job was terminated, he only desired to pursue yet another minister position. He gave a candidate sermon at a church in South Gate or Compton and sought to acquire that ministerial position which had been recently vacated, but the board voted against him after his one and only candidate sermon. He then immediately applied for a minister position in a community church in Palmdale and presented a candidate sermon there also. I accompanied him when he preached there on a Sunday morning. The leader in the church asked me to play the piano for the morning service, which I did. They agreed to vote and give him their decision that same afternoon. Anxious to learn if he had been accepted, we stopped at a pay phone on our way driving home and called regarding their decision. Unfortunately, they said that they had voted against him. Our children were being tossed around, moved from house to house and from church to church. They were very young and really did not understand the complexities of our lives.

Finally, disregarding our agreement, Dale secured another assistant minister position with Dr. George Peek at the North Long Beach Brethren Church late in May of 1961. This meant still another move. We rented a house on the corner of Poinsettia and Sixty-Third Street in Long Beach. Since the birth of David, Dale had become obsessed with wanting a vasectomy so there could never be a possibility of another child. He seemed to panic and wanted to schedule the surgery as soon as possible. He scheduled his appointment with a doctor in Lakewood, California, where he learned that it was mandatory for both the husband and the wife to be present; and furthermore, he had to have my signed consent in order for any doctor to perform the vasectomy. I refused to sign the consent form for many months for several reasons. First, I had read that many men who had a vasectomy suffered emotional problems afterward. I felt that he was not a good candidate for this surgery, and I really didn't want him to take the risk. Additionally, I still wished for a fourth child to make our family complete. Finally, I realized that he was so emotionally upset about my refusal to sign the consent that it couldn't be much worse to sign it and let him have his way. I went to his next doctor appointment and dutifully but reluctantly signed the papers. Now his vasectomy was scheduled to be performed during the week that we moved to his new job in North Long Beach. Things did not go well. However, he made excuses for not being able to work during that first week. Additionally, I noticed almost a sense of mourning in his personality, almost as if someone very close to him had died. I discovered later from reading additional research about vasectomies that a symptom of mourning, as if a close family member had died, often followed that surgical procedure and that mourning period could last for several months, in which his did.

Lacking one year for the completion of my Bachelor of Arts degree and a California lifetime teaching credential, I enrolled at California State University at Los Angeles, graduating with that degree in August of 1963. During that time, our children were settled in a public school a block away from our home, Curtis in third grade, Cathy in first, and David in the public preschool attached to that school playground. This was a good opportunity for me to attend college while they were all in school. An added incentive was the fact that David had entered the "terrible two" stage, and he was having a difficult time being the youngest and wanting to do things that he was not physically ready to handle. He would scream, have a tantrum, and throw himself on the floor at the slightest provocation. If I read a story to the two older children, he would scream and would not even settle down when I gave him 100 percent of my attention. I noted that he became a model child whenever he visited the preschool a block away, so I reasoned that if he was happy and could be such a model child there, I would take advantage of that opportunity and return to college myself. Additionally, during that period, I directed the children's choir at the church and took a leadership role in the Women's Ministry. I also became friends with many of the families in the church. We were a little more financially secure in this ministerial position so that we could finally pay our rent, buy food and clothing for our family, and be able to allow me to attend college and finish my coursework.

I secured a teaching position and began teaching a second-grade class in September of 1963 at the Willow School in Artesia, California. I received my first check on October 1; and that day I was excited as I drove home, entered through the back door, and walked into the kitchen. It seemed quiet in the house, but as I entered the living room to announce that I had finally received my first paycheck, I noticed that Dale was sitting on the couch with a very solemn look on his face. I took one look at him and almost instinctively knew what had happened, and I said, "You haven't been fired again, have you?" He said that it was true. This seemed to be the worst thing that had happened yet. After a few days of trying to figure out what had happened, I went directly to Dr. Peek and insisted on knowing the reason for Dale's abrupt termination. He said that the board had actually voted five months earlier in May to terminate him, but since we had three children and I was attending college, they would wait until the first day when I would receive a check; and they would plan to give his notice on that day. I could never have dreamed of such turbulence and mental torture as was ahead in our marriage. How could our loving relationship, our devotion to God, and our willingness to serve Him for our whole lives be turned upside down? How could my commitment to serve my husband as a Christian serves God, be broken or even destroyed? In spite of our differences, we had a marriage that seemed solid and actually was the envy of all of our friends. Our love seemed so deep that I could not even imagine ever living without him. This simply could not happen to us. We wouldn't let it happen. We would try everything possible to solve our dilemma.

CHAPTER 19

DIVORCE WORSE THAN DEATH

Remember the church in Compton where the board had voted against Dale after his one and only candidate sermon on a Sunday-morning sermon about two years earlier? Well, after Dale's sudden termination at the North Long Beach Brethren Church on October 1, 1963, there was three months of deadening silence from the church board or any of the church members. Thanksgiving festivities continued at the church, but we were not included or invited. Christmas came and we never as much as received a single Christmas card or a phone call from anyone at the church. We were living about five blocks away from the church. We had been so totally involved in the ministry and the church community, including all of their many activities for nearly two years, that it was almost impossible to believe that we were now complete strangers or outcasts. It was almost as if we no longer existed? It was extremely painful.

Dale felt the need for some resolution to this dilemma. He became involved in a therapy group which was organized by two Christian psychologists in Downey. He also had begun complaining of pain in his head and his back. Sometimes he would walk the floor for hours during the night due to pain. The therapy sessions twice a week were expensive, but I supported him in his search for answers to questions as to why he was losing his jobs and why he was having so much pain.

Dale decided just prior to Christmas that he wanted to go back to Iowa to visit his family and relatives. I thought that would be a fine idea. He said that he would purchase a plane ticket and then place a bomb on the plane. I was horrified at the very words that came out of his mouth. Yes, he was having emotional problems due to the loss of job after job and yes, he was beginning to have a lot of pain in his head and in his back; but putting a bomb on a plane and taking the lives of innocent people? Surely, he couldn't mean it. I tried hard to hold my emotions calm. I reasoned that he couldn't possibly think of such an idea. After all, he was the one who was petrified of guns, war, being killed, and dying. Additionally, he had no mechanical knowledge of physics or gunpowder; he couldn't possibly be involved in such a plot. I remained as calm as anyone could possibly be under these circumstances and assured him that I thought it would be best for him to go ahead and take a vacation where he could visit his family and friends. I agreed to organize his resume and call for an application so that he could obtain a California teaching credential. I also offered to arrange a substitute teaching position for him which could begin the first week of February. He did go on his trip to Iowa—uneventfully—and I never shared his threats and comments with anyone. I'm not sure, to this very day, that he knew what he was saying or that he would even remember his desperation and emotional reactions during that period.

After he returned from his trip in early January, he received a surprise call from Dr. George Peek, the minister who had fired him on October 1. Now remember that there had been complete silence from anyone for over three months. Seemingly out of the clear blue Dr. Peek told him that he would like to have him accept a position at a Brethren Church in Compton that had a parsonage next door to the church where our family could move immediately. When I returned from work, Dale seemed optimistic and stated that he was ready to accept this position. "Would I go with him?" he asked. I was much more reserved in my reaction but told him that I would pray about it and would let him know in the morning. I always believed that I made better decisions if I had time to pray and sleep on the idea. The morning came, and I was hurrying. The children had already left for school, and I had only a few minutes until I needed to leave. He approached me in the kitchen and asked what my answer was going to be. Calmly and quietly, I reminded him of our agreement wherein he would go into a different career if he were to lose another ministerial job. I also reminded him of the fact that he had already preached a candidate sermon at that same church where they voted against him less than two years prior. I said that he could accept the position and become the minister there if he wanted to, but I was not willing to quit my job, move the children again, and move into their parsonage; therefore, my answer would be no. Nothing in my background could ever have prepared me for his sudden outburst of cursing and swearing at me. He called me swear words out of the gutter that I had never heard in my whole life. He said that I was nothing but "dung" in his life. I became limp all over but regained enough strength to turn and walk out the door. I made no further comments about his outburst. I drove to my school and taught all day, but the encounter really caused me to feel heaviness in my heart. It seemed that everything I had done in our relationship, marriage, and in the ministry which I had believed was of Christian service was now in precarious danger of failure. I would still try to please and reconcile with him for yet another three years.

Within a month or two, I had completed the paperwork in order for him to obtain his California teaching credential, and I made a contact regarding a substitute-teaching position as I agreed. I spoke to the principal of the junior high school near where I was teaching in Artesia, California. By the end of January in 1964, the ABC Unified School District offered Dale a social studies or history substitute-teaching position in seventh and eighth grades. Fortunately, this position was a perfect match for his interests in history and his style of teaching. He had a rather difficult time with classroom management and discipline for the first few months, but he soon loved his teaching position.

Dale's therapy sessions continued over the next three years. The psychologists spoke with me frequently. They had already told me that I should expect Dale to relive all the stages of his life while in therapy, but I was not prepared for him to literally act as if he were a young boy, then a teenager for some time, and then as a young man trying to talk to me as he would have in order to prove his manhood to his own mother. This was all quite foreign to me, but I talked with his doctors and even participated in one or two of his therapy sessions. Later on in his therapy program, he became involved with a number of women in his sessions and eventually began coming home at 2:30 to 3:00 a.m. after his evening sessions. Many things started happening of which I would not want to tell anyone about. Now our children began crying because their father began acting in an irrational manner in their presence. I tried to persuade him to enter the

Long Beach Veteran's Hospital and seek psychiatric care. I even drove there with him where he began the preliminary interviews and screening. He was literally shaking and scared to death to talk to the doctors, and he refused any treatment or medication. He had even refused to take the medication which had been prescribed for him when he was treated earlier that year at the White Memorial Hospital in Pasadena, where he had been diagnosed with frequent and continuing petit mal seizures. We did not have insurance to cover his therapy or any private doctors, so I hoped that he would take advantage of his free medical treatments which were available to him at the VA Hospital in Long Beach. At least all expenses would be covered there. I also literally begged him to rent a room and live outside our home until he could feel better and could get control of his emotions. He did rent a room nearby for a few months, but one afternoon he came to our home and unexpectedly grabbed me off the couch in our living room, carried me into the bedroom, threw me on the bed, commanded me to submit to him, saying that it is written in the Bible that a wife should submit to her husband. As he placed both of his hands around my neck, I felt my very life was in danger. He had threatened the children previously but had continued being loving and supportive of me with only a few exceptions prior to that moment. My mind raced. I feared that I would not live to raise our children. He told me that he wanted to marry someone else who would know what it meant to submit as the Bible says. I froze and began to panic. Who would raise our children if I didn't live? He had been in no condition to even be around them without hurting or scaring them for nearly three years. How could he be such a gentle, compassionate minister one minute and then be so out of control the next minute? He had always insisted on his demands being met throughout most of our marriage. If he didn't get his way, he would accuse me of being cold or frigid. There certainly were times when I had been ill or was preparing for final exams for my college courses that I was not as available to him. Now while he was in therapy, he began making more excessive demands on command. One morning he demanded time with me while I was making oatmeal for the children, or he indicated that he would be unable to go to work. He seemed extremely desperate. I knew that he had been at his therapy session the evening before and didn't arrive home until three o'clock in the morning. Upon questioning him he readily admitted that he had been necking with the women in his therapy group so they could all get their emotions out in the open. Now only three hours later he was making demands of me. I called his doctors later that same day about this situation and asked them how I should handle it. His doctor asked me why I thought complying with his demands would help him get better. Then his doctor asked me, why was I continuing to respond to those types of demands? I needed clarification desperately. I asked how long the doctors were predicting that he would need therapy. I asked if they thought that he would ever have normal emotional reactions again. One day when Dale was having angry reactions and I was ready to call for help, he ripped the telephone wires out of the wall. I was devastated and finally asked if he wanted me to give him a divorce for a Christmas present. He said nothing, but his answer was clear to me; and I proceeded to find a lawyer and begin what turned out to be a five-year process of court cases, horrendous expense, and emotional upheavals. I never wanted a divorce from him and certainly did not want one at this time, but living under these conditions, I was finding my own life in jeopardy. I cried and prayed for guidance night and day for weeks. Finally, it become crystal clear to me that all of his actions for the previous three years which had pointed to an increased level of anger, hostility and threats toward the children were now pointed toward me. I was able to cope with the hostilities toward the children; but when his physical hostilities turned against me personally, I cried, shrank in fear, and could not handle it. The psychologists told me that when someone is suffering emotionally such as he was, they often turn against the person who is the closest to them. When I begged him to move out and get medical and psychiatric treatment, I was hoping that he would do just that. Instead, in his anger, he began spreading rumors amongst my teaching peers. He became extremely jealous that I carpooled to California State University in Los Angeles on Saturday mornings for a graduate class with another female teacher. She and I each taught fourth grade in classrooms next to each other for a year, and we both had to take the required research class which was offered at CSULA that year.

This was really becoming a nasty fight. Was he now trying to destroy my career also? After all, I had helped him apply for his teaching credential and even arranged for a substitute-teaching position in the same district where

I was teaching, so why would he now try to jeopardize my employment? Compounded with my feelings of hurt and dismay, I now was encountering many friends of mine who favored him and his representations about our marriage problems. People in the Lakewood Baptist Church were asking me how long it was going to take for me to get back together with him. Comments were floating around out there that I must have found someone else and therefore I had dumped him. I never felt so alone, so misunderstood, and so rejected by my fellow Christians. I had no idea that things could get even worse. I didn't know how cruel things could get until the children began having weekend visitations with him.

At the time of our separation, David was three, Cathy was six, and Curtis was eight. There had never been such an air of relief as the day when Dale moved out. I could not believe the tremendous relief to my emotional psyche and my daily workload. Since the day of our marriage, I had routinely picked up his clothing from the floor, drained the water from his bathwater, etc. Money which was deposited in the bank seemed to disappear before the end of each month. There were many times when our checking account became overdrawn. If the lawnmower sputtered and wouldn't start, he would proceed to purchase another. It was the same with his car. If it didn't work, then he wanted to push it across the street to the gas station and ask the mechanic on duty to fix it no matter what it cost. I personally never had any confidence in the mechanic at local gas stations. I didn't think they would be the most qualified to make automobile repairs. Whenever I told him that there was not enough money in the bank for him to write a check, he would become angry and say that I wasn't his mother and he would do whatever he wanted anyway. His personality had completely changed since the day he lost his last ministerial position. All the things that he said and did during that period were out of character for him. I do not believe that he was accountable for his thoughts or actions. Could this also be the post traumatic syndrome resulting from his war experiences? It was as if he was suffering from some unknown illness by which he was unable to be himself; nonetheless I had to make decisions regarding what was happening in real life. At this point in time, our real life relationship did not seem sustainable.

After filing for the divorce and after he was served with papers, he came out fighting, refusing to pay even one dollar of alimony or any child support if he could help it. He said that he was afraid that the judge would give me preferential treatment if I even smiled once in court. The judge had already stated during the divorce settlement that he had never handled a divorce where there was no community property to divide. Whatever pieces of furniture we had were from a damaged cargo outlet store or had been given to us. The only piece of furniture that we had of any value was the piano which my parents had given me at the time I graduated with my master's degree from California State University at Los Angeles. Dale demanded from the courts that he be given visitation every other weekend. That, in my opinion, became the most damaging thing that could ever have happened to our children at that time. They begged not to go with him, and then he accused me of poisoning their minds. After the children returned from their visitations, they were extremely upset emotionally. I decided to give them a choice—they could choose to live with Dale permanently, and I would not bother them for visitations unless they desired to spend time with me; but if they chose to live with me, they could not bring bad attitudes home and take them out on me. They finally agreed to treat me with decency after their return from visitations.

Dale finally moved into an apartment with a tall blond gentleman. The two of them set up housekeeping together and shared their new responsibilities with a great amount of dedication and respect for each other. One of them would shop for groceries, and the other one would cook and clean and do the dishes he told me proudly. The respect and admiration which they had for each other was obvious. One day Dale called and asked if he could borrow my cake mixer because he wanted to bake a birthday cake for his room mate's birthday that evening. I knew immediately that he was wearing a different persona. By comparison, he had only recognized my twenty-second birthday with a gift soon after our wedding, much less ever baking a cake. What a change! He had always said that I didn't need to be propped up as I already had too high of an opinion of myself, which I interpreted to mean that I had self confidence. I recalled so many demeaning comments that he made to me over the years that it actually began to sink in. I could no longer look the other way and try to ignore his comments or my reactions as if they had not been said. I became determined to ignore his demeaning accusations and concentrate on growing spiritually and healing emotionally. It was a long road paved with tears and many prayers. I had only cried once in my life prior to this experience, and that was when my new little collie puppy was hit by a car and killed. Struggling with death at the early age of eight, I now found the same helpless feelings encompass me regarding my failed marriage, humiliation, embarrassment, and loneliness. The difficulties in raising and disciplining three children alone seemed insurmountable. Even though I felt that I had actually shouldered the majority of the household tasks, working, and managing the family workload by myself for all the years I had been married, it was suddenly different when there was a negative force affecting us at all times for many years to follow. I had the distinct feeling that divorce was much worse than death. Death is final; there are no further arguments, court cases, and reactions as one parent pitted everything against the other. It is the most destructive thing that can happen to a marriage or to the children involved. There cannot be such a thing as a happy divorce.

Nearly five years into the divorce proceedings, Dale came to my home and said that he wanted to talk to me. He said that he had no memory of what happened in our marriage which could have led to a divorce. He asked me what happened? This would not have been a simple answer; however, I believed him in that he did not recall a single detail during those turbulent years and might only then have been awakening out of his apparent nightmare. I don't know much about amnesia, but if he was suffering from that disease no one ever diagnosed his illness or attempted to treat him properly. Years later I wondered if he actually had been suffering a relapse from post traumatic syndrome from his war experiences or could it have been from his impending brain tumor which was silently growing in his brain and was soon to be discovered? Nonetheless, he married soon after the divorce was final and made a full recovery after his brain tumor ruptured only moments prior to his scheduled brain surgery. He went on to live a very normal life endearing himself to our three children, outliving his second wife and eventually meeting a young Asian nurse who became "the love of his life", as he told us when we visited him in Leisure World. Her love and adoration quickened his steps and seemingly overshadowed his last few years here on this earth.

CHAPTER 20

SINGLE IN THE CAREER WORLD

After several months, I began to accept dates. I learned that almost without exception, men who had been married and divorced were more interested in instant gratification than in developing a relationship. Thus began a successive string of relationships which always ended in frustration. I finally told my father that I didn't believe that there was any man in my generation who were like men from previous generations; therefore, I was going to quit dating. His remark was quite interesting. He said, "You know that you can do anything that you need to do in life. You have made it on your own, and you really don't need a man in your life." Those were not the words that I wanted to hear, but I thought about it and realized that what he said was very true. I had learned to become self-sufficient, earn a good living, and support my family.

There were many times in my career when I would meet a secret or undercover predator face-to-face. One morning in Sacramento, I was ready to leave for a meeting at the capitol. A gentleman who was also on the same committee as I was called and said he was leaving for the meeting and would stop by and walk to the meeting with me. I really didn't know this person and was surprised by the call; however, since he was on our committee, I didn't think there was anything unusual. It was eight o'clock in the morning when he knocked on my door. There was only fifteen minutes' time until the meeting was to begin. I picked up my coat and proceeded to walk to the door. When I answered the door, he forcibly edged inside the door, shut the door, and instantly picked me up and forced me onto the bed, where he began to pull at my clothing. Fortunately, I was able to resist, and in a loud and stern voice I told him that this was not appropriate. He backed off and suddenly acted as if it never happened and proceeded to walk to the meeting with me. I distanced myself emotionally from any friendly communication or encounters with this person, and I was able to complete the assigned work without further confrontations. I certainly learned that I should never let my guard down and that a woman is always vulnerable to the whim of any male predator and male predators are not distinguishable from other more honest and gentler men.

Another situation happened at an administrator's training conference which was held at the California State University Kellogg campus in Pomona. Every administrator in our district was required to attend this all-day Saturday conference. At that time, I was a director of the reading-specialist program in Cerritos, California, and was assigned as assistant principal to one of two principals who were sharing our same school office. The principal I was assisting was Tom Gallagher, and I was happy to perform as much of his workload as possible because I was working toward a promotion to a principal position. The other principal, a Hispanic man, was new to our school that year. Both of these administrators plus my reading-specialist program supervisor, Hal Barsh, attended that conference.

During a break between sessions in the afternoon, the Hispanic principal told us he had just purchased a new home near this campus, and he invited five of us to see his new home. He was so proud of his first home that he insisted that we see it. Each of us agreed to accompany him to his house a mile or two away. By the time we were to meet in front of our conference center, the other four persons had changed their minds one by one. I was already there, and when I found out that they were not coming, I wanted to change my mind also but felt that would have been rude since I was already there. I called out to Mr. Barsh and gestured to him that I would only be gone fifteen minutes, and if I wasn't back by then, that they should come after me. I had no reason to suspect that this administrator who worked every day out of the same office as I did would deadbolt the front door to his door after I entered his house, place his keys on the counter, take a swig of what looked like whiskey, and then immediately throw me onto the floor and thrust his full two hundred pounds on top of me and begin attempting to rape me. The shock was so sudden that I was hardly able to think, but fighting and resistance got me nowhere, so I mentally decided to feign cooperation and pray that I would be able to catch him off guard and make my escape. I could see that there were several guns on the floor less than ten feet away from me, and I became nearly paralyzed with fear. He was very heavy on top of me and had jammed his tongue down my throat, choking me and making it impossible for me to scream; but the second that I began to fake cooperation, he relaxed just long enough for me to wrestle away, run to the kitchen, grab his car keys, and then rush frantically to the door. He had been unsuccessful in a rape, and now he was angrily staggering toward me. I finally reached out for the door only a half second ahead of him, unlocked it, and ran for his car. He was coming right behind me as I opened his car, got inside, and locked the door. He pounded on the door and window, begging me to open the door. I tried the key in the ignition, but the car would not start. I was shaking and fumbling as I tried repeatedly to start his car. His home was surrounded by orange groves, and the only other house next door appeared to be vacant. I thought of trying to run, but I didn't know where I was and probably would not be able to outrun him. Finally, as time stood still, I decided to reason with him. I rolled down the window slightly, put on my most commanding voice, and told him that he must tell me how to start his car. Finally, he said that he would not hurt me if I would let him in and he would drive the car himself. I told him that I had instructed Mr. Barsh to come after me if I wasn't back in fifteen minutes and the time was up and he should be coming immediately for me. Finally, knowing that he had guns available and that I must make the best decision possible, I let him drive his car. He turned a different switch than I ever knew about on a car, started it, and drove back to the conference center. During that five- to ten-minute drive, he constantly tried to pull my hair, grabbed at my clothing, and drove in an erratic manner. I constantly prayed under my breath and kept commanding him as to how he should drive. Obviously, he was drunk by now; and when I arrived at the conference center feeling limp and disheartened, I sat on the steps of the conference center as close to all of my fellow administrators as I could as if for their protection from a madman who was there in our midst. I tried to make small talk, but that failed. One person asked me if I was all right, and I said yes since I did not want to make a full explanation at that time.

The next morning I made an appointment with the superintendent of schools for that district. I reported the full episode to him and said that I did not believe that we should have a rapist working in our district. I wanted a police report, but the superintendent said, "You know that if we report this that the police and everyone in the district would think that you are lying or that you really propositioned him and that he was probably merely trying to please you. Your reputation will be destroyed if you try to report him to the police." I held back tears and pled with him. I told him that probably the next person might be killed, and the next person might even be his own wife. All my comments made no impression on him, so I continued on my job, making a great effort to keep a distance from this individual for the remainder of that school year. He continued his employment with no police or legal action taken against him.

There were other times when the seemingly most professional of administrators or governmental personnel tried equally conniving attacks as the one I just described. I began to believe that all men had only their own personal gratification on their minds. I became extremely overcautious in my dealings with men. And it wasn't just men; I was even solicited by a female classroom teacher as well as by a lady who was a professor in college. Working in government positions, I was beginning to have firsthand experience of the degeneration of our culture and the low moral standards to which our present generation seemed to be sinking.

When I listen to the news and hear about rapes and murders of young girls and even mature women, I can personally vouch for how easily those situations can happen. Young girls or even women of any age could never be cautious enough. Our lives can literally be hanging in the balance at any street corner, at any public meeting, in any parking lot, or at any shopping center. One must always be on guard. I wish we could warn young girls and even older women about the dangers of rape and its serious consequences especially from men who appear to be upstanding and friendly.

Young girls and even some women dress in such a provocative manner as to actually entice men to become aroused at the skin or cleavage which they reveal. It really is no wonder that there are so many rapes and murders of female victims. I do not believe that girls intentionally want attention from men; however, they are definitely teasing men by their scant dress, showing skin, and enticing behavior. Obviously they have not learned their lessons the hard way, or they would not be so daring in their dress. Girls and women who learn these lessons the hard way often do not live to tell their story. The nightly news is full of examples of beautiful college girls who disappear only to be found dead days, weeks, months, or even years later. This is not a scare tactic on my part to mention these dangers, but I want to caution every girl to cherish her life, be discreet in her apparel and genuine in her personality. Every encounter has the potential for either danger or possibly a wonderful relationship. Each person must be the commander of his or her own ship and pray for divine guidance every hour and every day of his or her life.

There are many warnings in the Bible which assist us in taking heed in how to live our life. Chapter 2 of Proverbs is a good example of moral guidelines which can benefit us in these areas of our lives.

Chapter 21

Overcoming Poverty

The very first day after the divorce proceedings were started, I sat down with the children and explained how important it is to understand money. It takes money to buy everything we need. We can waste our money on candy, soda, and popcorn or we can save every penny. Every dime saved is a dime earned and we must find as many ways as possible to earn money and quickly invest it so that it can be working for us making even more money. It was a very critical moment and a turning point for us as a family. Essentially, we would be starting all over again at the very beginning, but this time we were going to be able to earn and save enough money to be able to purchase things that we needed. We were still renting and living in an older Dutch farmhouse where we had lived since 1963.

Soon the children each began finding ways to earn money. Curtis and David went through the trash almost every night in the back of the local bicycle store and brought home discarded bicycle parts which they cleaned up and assembled and finally built several near-new-looking bicycles. They were able to sell each bike for anywhere from $50-$100. They even built a bicycle for their grandfather out of the parts they found. They shined every piece of metal and painted the bicycle a grass-green color. Their grandfather was extremely surprised and excited about their gift. Additionally, the children sold Christmas napkins by going door-to-door. In the late spring after the strawberry pickers abandoned their fields, which were near my job, the children picked the remaining strawberries in the field and sold the newly boxed strawberries to our neighbors.

After we bought our home on Heather in 1968, it was nearly another year until we were able to purchase our first new automobile. We picked a dark green Plymouth station wagon. We were so excited to take a drive to a lovely beach in Corona del Mar. The children were pleased and impressed to have a new car and to learn how saving and using money wisely were important lessons.

Saving money became very important. Each of the children found ways to earn money, and they watched as the interest paid by the bank helped their money grow. Lessons learned at such a very early age has given them a financial benefit throughout their lifetimes. Never did we have an allowance given to the children; however, after they managed to do some work that made a difference in our home or our family, they often received money for their efforts.

Personally, I believe that allowances which are given simply because that child was born into a particular family teaches those children that everything should be given to them, and therefore when they are ready for college, they expect all their expenses to be paid. Later in life, those same individuals expect the government to give them and their children free education, free health care, free housing, etc.

I could not be certain, but I wonder if successful business entrepreneurs were raised as children to believe that their own hard work alone would lead to their success, earning their own college tuition, and starting their own businesses. Success and financial rewards might parallel the gifts which they received as a child after completing a project which would benefit the whole family.

It might be a great research project to compare children who received allowances against those who were expected to contribute to the family whether or not they were rewarded. This subject is certainly worthy of further thought and exploration.

CHAPTER 22

CON ARTISTS

Some people said they thought that I led a sheltered life, but I thought that they were wrong. However, when it came to recognizing lying, deceit, and double lives, I was the last to figure things out. If that means that I was sheltered, then I concede. Looking back, my first marriage had elements of deceit which I attempted to overlook and tried to make the best of a situation, but every problem kept coming back to haunt me. As a matter of fact, I now believe that one can never outlive wrong turns in the road. The best that one can hope and pray for is to relinquish those wrong choices by giving them over to our Heavenly Father, admit the mistake, ask forgiveness, and get up and take a new step in the right direction. It is my prayer that recounting some of my experiences would serve to help someone else make right choices in their life. I am reluctant to discuss many of my experiences; however, I have felt led to share my stories in an effort to save someone else from suffering some of the consequences which I have suffered. Clearly, we need more wisdom in making choices in life and on how to protect ourselves.

I met a new friend when I visited a Sunday-school class for singles. I'll call him Tim, which was not his real name. He was well educated, polished with a PhD from Princeton, an avowed Christian, an author and illustrator, divorced with three children. His deep resonating voice attracted everyone to him; and he seemed compassionate, considerate, talented, and energetic. Beneath the surface of this attractive personality was a hidden personality of fear, loathing, retaliation, mental anguish, a depth of despair which ultimately caused him to commit suicide. Unknowingly, my life was always in danger when I dated him. I'm not sure how anyone could have determined the depth of his troubled mind. He was well-known, friendly, and on the surface seemed very honest, normal, and trustworthy.

Another suitor, we'll call him Rob, was from a most prominent family heavily involved in church leadership. This person seemed to have an air of perfection in personality, talent, leadership, Christianity, and craftsmanship. He was a perfectionist at courting, saying the politically correct things, and giving the most meaningful gestures and gifts. Lurking beneath this façade was a personality of greed, sneaking, lying, stealing, and ultimately control tactics. If the underlying personality were never to be found out, he might survive in a relationship in which he held all the cards and could have complete control. Were any card to crumple, disaster would surely follow. I should have been able to identify and understand the inherent dangers in spending any time with this person; however, I did spend innocent time with him and felt betrayed and emotionally burned as soon as I began to see through his charade.

Reflecting on my first marriage, I now believe he was driven predominately by his own personal needs. I thought that I understood his needs and that I could help to nurture and build a successful marriage with him. I was not entirely blind, but I thought he would mature and we could have a stable marriage. Satisfying a needy person would take a lifetime of selfless service as I found out, and it is humanly impossible to win in an incompatible situation. Not fully recognizing his underlying needs led me to believe that time would bring about maturity. I felt that with prayer and God's help, I could manage to help him with all of his needs. Certainly I thought that he possessed enough good qualities necessary for a relationship so that we could build a successful marriage. I did not realize that the needy portion of this person could never be filled and there actually was a flipside to his personality. When I finally learned that one human being can never fulfill all the needs of another person, I felt as if I were a complete failure. I never knew the relationship was doomed from the start even though there were more than ten years where we carved out some semblance of happiness, brought three children into the world, and tried my hardest to build a strong and a solid marriage. It takes both parties to pull together as a team to make a relationship work.

There was also another friend whom I met who had worked as government CIA agent. He probably had the highest intelligence quotient of any person I had ever met. He spoke eight languages fluently, was experienced in espionage and high-level dignitary duties, honored in our country, and was expert in courting. This person I soon found had two distinct personalities. He was a deeply religious Catholic, well educated, wealthy, polished, creative, with a legal mind on one hand; but he actually had a diametrically opposite personality hidden well below the surface. That other personality, which was rarely seen by the public or even by members of his own family, was rebellious against all laws, a complete atheist, always felt poverty ridden, was same-sex oriented and cleverly deceitful in nature. How does one uncover the hidden personalities of a supposedly devoted friend when his association with me turned out to cleverly allow him access and credibility within my educational circles? He needed an association with me in order to make certain contacts in the educational and political world which he desperately needed. I soon realized that I was being used for his personal and future business success. It was a little like having a leech attaching itself to you. These were the kinds of issues which I began to deal with as a single person who was considered successful in the educational, business, and financial world.

Perhaps one more experience will help summarize the dozens of situations which I encountered in risking the development of any new relationships. There was another person whom I admired greatly. He was in my statistics class in the master's program at the university. This was a very difficult course, and I had been indoctrinated in my undergraduate courses in the Midwest to believe that African people were not very intelligent. It was to my amazement when this African American student seemed to be the most brilliant person in this class. I sat there wondering how it was possible that an African American person could obviously be more intelligent than everyone else in that class. Later in group discussions, I became acquainted with him. He seemed to have a radiant personality, was interested in assisting with those of us who were having difficulties in that course. We met for lunch. Later he asked to give my children a tour of the college campus. They also enjoyed his sense of humor and his keen and personal interest in their aspirations. He was a very charismatic person who possessed leadership qualities which could assist him to rise to the level of becoming a high-level political candidate if he so chose. He was married with children of his own but would have thrown all that away in order to gain a white woman on his arm in public. His hidden agenda was to use my acquaintance or friendship as a means of extortion. For example, he would find it necessary to fly to different Southern states for family emergencies, call me on the phone, and demand that I immediately wire hundreds of dollars to him or else he would have some crisis which could never be solved without those funds. The decision to say no to someone who had befriended my family was a tough decision for me to make because I was gullible enough to believe that I could help everyone especially when it was a return favor to a person who had helped me in my college class. I did make the decision to say no, which instantly severed any further friendship and also relieved me from being used for further extortions.

Being a con artist with a hidden agenda is not exclusively a man's province; I have known of a few women trying the same tactics. I have had many other similar situations. A con artist has actually developed his or her skills by testing the waters and then using every conniving trick in order to win the confidence of that person. We need to be wise, always on the alert, ready, and capable of making the right decision quickly. Con artists are everywhere in this world. Happy, successful single females are especially sought out by con artists. It shouldn't take a lifetime to learn all the deceitful ways in which these men and women operate. Perhaps there should be a course in high school, in the local churches, or even at the community-college level. Perhaps being accused of living a sheltered life really meant that I was naive to the hidden intentions or personality irregularities in people that I met and with whom I might have been sucked into trying to build a lasting friendship.

It is critically important to make the right decisions at every turn and crossroad in life. Each person is only given one life to live, and it passes by very quickly. Young people often believe they are indestructible and will live forever. They think they can do anything without repercussions or consequences. Once they have an accident or make a big mistake, it can never be reversed.

Recently I attended the funeral of the grandson of one of my former teachers. He was her only grandson, and he was showered with more love and affection by his family and friends than most teenagers are. He was vacationing at his grandmother's home for the summer. A call came to his grandmother at about four o'clock early one morning, asking her to come and identify his body. His new truck was barely recognizable, and since he was not wearing his seat belt, he was thrown from his truck, which overturned and killed him instantly. He thought he was invincible. He was strong and had many close friends. What else could he want? It only took one accident and this eighteen-year-old lost his life. His many friends who attended his funeral were in shock. How could this happen to him? There was no second chance and no turning back. It is believed that he fell asleep while driving five miles to his grandmother's home after partying with his friends. He probably never knew what happened.

CHAPTER 23

PRESIDENT OF A STATEWIDE ORGANIZATION

After teaching second, fourth, fifth, and sixth grades in the ABC Unified School District for a total of five years, I became a reading-specialist teacher. This position provided me with the opportunity to create a cross-age tutoring program whereby students in fourth through sixth grades could guide and direct first, second, or third-grade students in many learning activities in a special classroom which I designed for this program. I had taken extra coursework in order to earn a reading specialist credential, and I was thoroughly enjoying this challenging teaching assignment.

During one of my training conferences, I was approached by Dr. Robert Acosta, who was the state of California director in the field of teaching reading. He indicated that he believed some of us were totally capable and could help improve the educational system in California. I thought about organizing teachers throughout the state in order to introduce legislation so we could bring about positive changes in the educational programs in California. Dr. Acosta was a very dedicated and well-educated man who certainly was trying his best to improve the educational system. He told me that he was the thirteenth child, born of a Spanish family in Mexico. I was impressed by his intelligence and keen sense of work ethics. I considered his advice and began working to organize about eighteen hundred reading-specialist teachers throughout California. I hired an attorney to develop a nonprofit organization which we named Reading Specialists of California. All these efforts began in

133

my home in the evenings after teaching a fourth-fifth combination class of thirty-two students all day. Near the spring of that school year, I was selected to become the consultant to represent the state department of California and department of education in Sacramento to supervise, train, and improve the teaching skills of reading-specialist teachers and the reading programs throughout Southern California. My duties were to supervise every Miller-Unruh Reading Specialist Program specifically in seven Southern counties. It also became my responsibility to coordinate a statewide program in coordination with Mr. Vincent Abata, who had been hired to supervise the reading programs for the central and northern counties. This job required a lot of flying back and forth to Sacramento, but I was usually able to limit my nights away from home to one or two nights during the middle of the week. Occasionally it was necessary to present large training conferences, and those projects required two overnights and three days on site at each of the designated locations.

At the end of this one-year term for the state of California, I was offered a position as a state coordinator of reading programs as well as for the state testing program. My new office was to be placed in Santa Ana, California.

I soon had another experience which turned out to be one of the most challenging experiences of my teaching career. As an educational consultant for the state of California, I was housed in the office of education in Orange County. I learned that in the case of a teacher strike anywhere in the public-school system of California, the employees of the state educational offices would be immediately assigned to substitute for the teachers who were on strike. Therefore, on one beautiful morning I was met at work by the assistant superintendent of Orange County office of education and told that on this day I would be assigned to teach six consecutive classes of advanced algebra to high school students in a predominantly black high school in the south side of Santa Ana. This was my first experience of teaching in a situation where the teachers were marching on strike just outside open windows of their respective classroom. I found the students I was assigned to teach to be rowdy, rude, loud, and rebellious. Many of the boys were large, muscular, seniors, and on the football team. I thought that I could surely appeal to the students to sit down and give their attention to me; however, that was not what happened. The first thing I did was to close the windows and the doors in order to shut out some of the noisy chanting outside. No sooner had I shut the windows than several boys went over to the windows and doors and opened them again. I thought that since I had never had a problem with discipline in teaching before, surely I must either gain control quickly or most certainly be seriously injured or possibly even be killed in such a riot. The students refused to sit down. One girl in the front seat was sitting on top of her desk facing the back of the room and watching the rowdy students. I gently and quietly appealed to her, touching her softly on the shoulder, and requesting that she sit in her desk. She yelled out at the top of her voice, "Don't touch me, my parents will sue you!" My mind raced, and not yet willing to admit defeat, I tried one more approach. "Is there anyone in this class who would be willing to be my teaching assistant for class today?" I asked, barely being heard above the ruckus. Three girls put up their hands, and now it was up to me to make a wise choice between them. I was definitely breathing a silent prayer as I contemplated as to who I thought the boys in the class would admire and respect enough to sit down and listen. I selected a small but pretty girl who was sitting near the back of the room. I called her forward and gave her instructions to relay to the class and immediately, as she spoke in her quiet and almost shy voice, a miracle happened. All the students became quiet and sat down in their desks to listen to her. I asked her to write the algebra problems on the chalkboard and to call on different students in the class to work the problem out loud while she wrote their answers on the board. She did a wonderful job, and I wrote a letter of commendation to the principal regarding her capabilities and qualities as my assistant for that class. Each of the five successive hours of teaching that day, I followed the same routine. Each of the assistants whom I selected was able to remarkably and calmly follow instructions in order to direct the class in their lessons and chalkboard presentations. I personally wrote a letter of commendation for each of the students who assisted me that day and mailed it to their principal. When the day was over, I was so thankful to have discovered a teaching technique which I believe saved my life. There had been no shortage of anger, hostility, and rage in those students that day. They could easily have over taken me, and I was well aware of their strength and power. One day of substitute teaching under those stressful conditions was enough for me. From that day forward, I have had the greatest respect as well as sympathy and understanding for teachers who are placed in such dangerous and compromising positions. There are many students who not only have no respect for their own parents but also carry that same attitude of arrogance, disrespect, and abhorrence into the classrooms. I was happy to return to my consultant position, but I will always empathize with teachers in crime-ridden schools who encounter unusual and dangerous situations such as that one turned out to be.

CHAPTER 24

FAMILY CRISIS

It was five o'clock on a Sunday morning, July 1 in 1975, when my telephone rang. I could hardly discern the man's voice who was urging me to go quickly to the hospital in Fallbrook where he had taken my father at 2:30 a.m. Finally waking up enough, I recognized the voice of the neighbor, Eric Scott, who lived next to the ten-acre ranch where my father was spending the weekend caring for his Black Angus cattle. Realizing the urgency in his voice, I managed to be out of the house in about fifteen minutes and arrived in record time at the Fallbrook Hospital, about 110 miles away. My mother was visiting family and friends in Minneapolis, Minnesota, at the time, and I knew that whatever care would be given my father would be my full responsibility. My father was extremely agitated to be in the hospital, was having trouble breathing as his lungs filled with fluid from an onset of congestive heart failure. As I entered his room, I detected that he was resisting all forms of treatment from the nurses who were trying to assist him. Gently, I encouraged him to cooperate so the doctors and nurses could diagnose his problem, treat his condition, and get him back to his ranch as soon as possible.

The ranch was fulfilling a zest for farming which ran deep in my father's blood. His hard work and long hours at the ranch were merely a change of pace for him from his full time work at the private school which he and my mother owned and managed in Long Beach. Wherever he was, he worked unbelievably long hours. At the private school during the week, he would traditionally arrive at the school at 4:00 to 4:30 a.m.

to complete his bookwork, clean and tidy the classrooms, and then greet the sleepy children as their mothers brought them to school as early as 6:00 a.m. As soon as teachers arrived to begin their day, he would be off to the wholesale stores by 7:00 a.m. to purchase the needed groceries for snacks and lunches. Then he would stop at the hardware store for parts in order to make repairs or build new playground equipment. After shopping at the paper-supply company, he would stop at the bank and return in time to begin cooking lunch for the children. After lunch, when the children were napping, he would disappear to his home nearby and catch a short nap in his backyard. Two hours later, he would return to school, where he was always working on a major project such as building a new patio roof, refinishing a boat which he bought to place on the playground for the children, or building a new play structure. On and on it went for the fifteen years my parents owned and managed the school.

There were many times when I had received a call from my mother asking me if I would consider managing their school for them, possibly even consider eventually purchasing it from them. My answer had always been an absolute no. I was so involved in my own educational career that I rarely ever even visited my parents' school more than a couple times during that fifteen-year period. I had, however, assisted them for that one time three-month period in 1960 when they first purchased the school. I did teach first grade for them and assisted with administering their elementary school program. At the time my father suffered his first congestive heart failure attack, I was totally happy with my consultant position with the state of California and my office in Santa Ana. I had no intention of ever changing my job or leaving the California public educational system.

Sizing up the enormous responsibilities of filling in for both of my parents at their private school, driving back and forth to monitor his medical condition, taking charge of the dozen or so cattle and their newborn calves on the ranch, I immediately called Dr. Petersen, the superintendent of Orange County schools and requested a one-year leave of absence. This was a very hard decision to make, but I was sure that I could return by the end of the year and my time would have been well spent.

Of course, one cannot always see into the future and plan their time so easily; however, my leave was granted, and now I only had one gigantic problem to solve. I knew in my heart of hearts that I personally had many diametrically opposite philosophical views on management of people, teaching techniques, business strategies, etc. How could I work within the system my parents had set up and yet be in a managerial position for a whole year? I needed to find a way to purchase the school and their business, but I did not have any money for even a down payment. Time was of the essence. Mother was out of town, Father was critically ill and obviously would not be able to ever work again, and there was no one else who could possibly step in and run the school at that time. Yes, there had been a gentleman who made an offer to purchase the school about six months prior, but he was intending to run it as an absentee owner. It turned out that he was planning a fraudulent business deal, and he actually ended up in jail a few months later. I started wondering if I were ever able to find a way to purchase the business; could I structure the business so that I could be the absentee owner at the end of my leave and then return to my job? It became my plan to do just that. First I had to figure out a way to borrow or find access to funds in order to make such a large purchase.

Three hundred thousand dollars was the firm price, and favors had never been made by my parents to any of their own three children. I visited the president of the bank to see if I could get a loan on this short timeline. Actually, I had to take over the school the very next day, and I had only met a couple of their employees briefly prior to that time. After much frustration with trying to convince a loan officer that I could run that business, I devised a plan whereby I would pay $7,000 down, make separate payments for the $43,000 remainder of the down payment, spread it over a three-year period, assume their first mortgage payments on one secured loan they had for $28,000, and amortize the remainder over a ten-year period. Those payments totaled nearly $6,000 per month. This was a superhuman undertaking which I was willing to commit to fulfilling. An attorney drew up the contract, and within ten days, both of my parents signed the contract. My father actually lowered the price by $50,000 at the last minute. Soon after this transaction was completed, my father began gaining some of his strength back. Within two months, my parents set off to enjoy their retirement, traveling and visiting with their many friends and relatives everywhere. They began enjoying the eighteen months my father had yet to live. My loan payments provided a sizeable monthly income for them from their sale of the school to me. From that fateful day, July 1, 1975, neither of my parents visited the school again or assisted with the transition. I did have a few questions about their ledger-style accounting system which my father had been using for the fifteen years which they owned the school. He briefly answered my questions but any questions about improving, updating, or expanding the business were always met with, "This is only a family business. Keep it that way, and don't try to make it into a commercial venture."

I learned quickly that if I were to survive financially, I would need to take the position of the opening person at 6:00 a.m., do the school laundry, become the cook, wash the dishes, cover the full twelve hours of business operation, and complete all accounting and bookwork evenings and weekends. Sixty hours a week was only the beginning because it usually amounted to eighty hours or more. I was determined to make it work.

My children were doing very well in their schools. David was in junior high, Cathy was in high school, and Curtis was in his first year at Long Beach City College. They had already become accustomed to my previous travel schedule when I worked for the state department, and they knew that I could always be reached by phone. The new circumstances really made no difference in their schedules of football practice, swimming meets, orchestra rehearsals, etc. I tried to make my time with them the highest quality I could. Obviously, we would not be able to take trips like the six-week trip to the East Coast we had taken two summers before, nor could we fly to Acapulco, Mexico, for a week as we had done together in the past summer in celebration of each of their graduations.

Now the scene changed quite dramatically, and it became necessary for me to call on my children and their friends to help me with the business on several occasions in order to make repairs, refurbish the school, or even assist with supervision of the summer-camp programs in the years to come.

Superhuman as I tried to be, the long hours, the stress, and financial burdens made me vulnerable to the Asian influenza which hit Southern California in the fall of 1975. Shortly before Thanksgiving, I was hit hard again with the flu virus, which lingered on and seemed to settle in the nerves surrounding my spinal cord. It was very similar to the flu which I had contracted in the fall of 1960. That was the year that I tried to help my parents in their newly purchased school. This time I was hospitalized in the Long Beach Community Hospital and was prescribed antibiotics and tranquilizing drugs in an effort to ease the severe pain in my spine. I literally seemed to lose touch with reality, felt that I could float or might not be able to stop myself from jumping out the second-story window. I became agitated very easily. I guess I sounded cross and angry, according to my family, when they went to visit me. Possibly this was all a result of pent-up feelings of being trapped with too heavy a financial burden. I believe that my parents may have helped my employees at the school during that period. However, I never was told how everyone managed to get through in my absence, but I was glad to overcome that illness and to return even stronger in my commitment to succeed.

Several other people were also stricken with that same particular strain of virus. A teller whom I visited with each time I went to the bank became ill the same week that I did, lapsed into a coma which lasted for a full year. Finally he regained consciousness, but he was never the same after that and certainly was never able to hold a banking position again. His return to health was attributed to the prayers and constant vigilance and stroking around-the-clock from his friends who stood by him for that whole year. When I saw him a year or two later, he looked a mere shadow of his former self, and I was reminded of how thankful I should always be to have regained my full health and strength.

Christmastime was nearing, and I was just getting back into the full swing of a twelve-hour workday. The idea of giving Christmas presents actually brought tears to my eyes as I struggled first to make all financial commitments regarding the school purchase, the business, and secondly to try to keep food on our table at home. I did not think I would be able to make it financially unless I could come up with a better strategy. I hired an accountant friend, Roy Henning, and asked him to look at my financial picture and make any suggestions he could which might help. He patiently mapped out the business income and all the expenses and made projections by which the business could become more profitable. His suggestions regarding spending a greater percentage of the income on advertising seemed an impossible task, but gradually I discovered that increasing my advertising brought more students and greater income, thereby making it easier to meet all financial obligations and finally have a few dollars left over for living expenses for our family.

By the beginning of spring, our student enrollment had increased from the forty-five students, which were there when I took over the school in July, to 125 the following spring. This not only helped my financial dilemma, but since that facility could only license for one hundred students, the influx of enrollees also encouraged me to purchase another building for the expansion of the schools. I barely had made ends meet by early January, but by June I thought I had enough reserve money in the bank for a $25,000 down payment on a building which came on the market at the end of June. It worked out perfectly. I purchased the new building on July 1, 1976; and my sons, Curtis and David, with the help of our contractor friend (George Shanks) and other friends worked on the conversion into a school building. After necessary renovations were made the school was ready to open by the 15 of October. The students were ready and anxious to move in, and they were thrilled with their new school building.

Remembering that my leave of absence expired on June 30, 1976, I requested an additional year of leave. My request was denied so as to not set a precedent. My decision at that time was whether to try to sell the school (which would have devastated my ailing father) or to expand, which had become necessary if I were to continue in the private-school business. The decision was clear; I needed to expand the business and venture further into the private-school business.

My reputation as a public-school teacher, administrator, consultant to the state department of California, and lobbyist testifying to the educational needs in the public schools represented my high standards. I would always need to excel if I were to stay in the private-school arena. I had become proficient in writing curriculum, tests, programs, legal documents, and legislation which were used for improvement in education, budgeting for educational programs at the state level; but I had never been involved with the day-to-day advertising for students, collecting of tuition, and paying bills for a private business. This part of the business I needed to learn quickly; my very survival as a business and property owner as well as a homeowner and head of a single-parent family all depended on my succeeding.

Growth and expansion were reaffirming, challenging, and exciting; but to my surprise, I had overlooked the fact that every penny of cash income would become taxable and the $25,000 which I thought I had in reserve in the bank turned out to be the exact amount which I would owe in income tax. Suddenly, I felt the pain of having to support the government with up to 50 percent of the net incoming tuition. When I was just beginning to feel comfortable with handling money in a totally different way, suddenly the business looked insurmountable. How could I manage a business, provide for growth and expansion when all the profit would need to be paid in taxes? Discouraged as I was, I now found myself trapped in the system. My leave of absence had expired; I was committed to the purchase of the additional building with high costs of refurbishing and an additional ten-year mortgage payment. Suddenly I had a new realization that income tax would take most of the profits. Overcoming this dilemma would become one of the greatest challenges yet in my life.

CHAPTER 25

LEGAL AND POLITICAL CRISIS

B ecoming politically active became important in order to make necessary changes within private schools so they could more adequately serve the needs of children in the state of California. There had been two separate organizations in California for nearly fifteen years. The preschool association of California was somewhat familiar to me as I had heard a few details from my parents who had each served a term as president of that association. They had been responsible for organizing workshops for preschool teachers in southern California, and I had been a guest at a couple of those workshops several years prior. Now I became involved in the preschool association, known as PSA. I eventually began lobbying and representing the needs of children in private schools in Southern California. I also organized training seminars for private-school administrators regarding writing bills to solve their educational problems as well as how to present their needs to senators and assemblymen. We hired a professional lobbyist whom I had worked with when I was representing the public-school reading teachers in the late 1960s. Having been active in Sacramento for five years for public education, I knew immediately how to contact legislators, representatives, and attorneys in order to get a job done. Having been personally responsible for forming a statewide nonprofit organization for the purpose of enacting legislation in 1969, I was ready and willing to see that fairness and improvement could readily be achieved for the private-school industry also.

Our school business continued to grow and expand. Training teachers became a large portion of the task; and in order to properly hire and train teachers, I found that I also had to present demonstrations, write and expand curriculum guides, booklets on teaching techniques, rules and regulations, etc. Since I was extremely busy training our own teachers, we decided to present our training program for other private-school teachers also. We utilized our two school campuses and included PSA members in our training sessions. This meant training hundreds of private preschool and elementary teachers as well as their directors, owners, and administrators. The demand was so great that I directed an intensive three-day training workshop for private-school administrators in Kauai, Hawaii, in 1980. The exciting concept of that workshop was the fact that I was able to recreate the teaching and learning style on the adult level that would awaken those educators to the real avenues of learning which are most successful in teaching children. Having a completely new environment in which administrators could learn a new language; go on field trips; observe new topography; and discover different kinds of birds, flowers, trees, and sea life than they were previously familiar with gave the opportunity to demonstrate, analyze, and outline teaching techniques that can happen in a real classroom setting. This turned out to be one of the most successful seminars I had ever had the opportunity to present.

An appointment was made by then governor George Deukmejian in 1984 for me to be placed as a committee member working on the Prevention of Child Molestation committee. This was a great honor; and I was truly experienced, capable, and ready to be of assistance in tackling this problem, which had become prevalent in California. It was in the newspapers everywhere that children had been molested in the McMartin Preschool in Redondo Beach. The stories that the five-year-old children allegedly told investigators were gruesome and unbelievable. Parents, however, began suing Mrs. McMartin and also her son for allegedly conspiring to dig underground caves under the preschool where they were reportedly molesting children.

You know the old saying, "Calm goes before a storm." Sometimes that can also be true in the business and educational world as well. Already, many changes and upgrades in curriculum and the expectations of our teachers had made an astounding difference in the success of our students.

The kindergarten program was especially popular with parents. Mr. Norm had his students reading fluently within the first two or three months of kindergarten. They were also writing essays, discussing world events, and intrigued with complex science lessons. Some of them chose to be in his musical drama productions. They literally enjoyed every minute of their classroom instruction—yet he was the teacher who was soon to be targeted in the copycat McMartin molestation lawsuit.

Now it happened that among the children attending our elementary school was a child, Julie,* who had transferred to us from the McMartin Preschool. Julie's mother told me confidentially that she knew that Julie had not been molested and she knew the McMartin family very well and she said that she was sure that none of the accusations were true. A few months later, another parent, Mrs. Smith,* enrolled her child, Christine,* in the same kindergarten class in our school. Mrs. Smith, who worked at the Perona Law Firm in Long Beach, had access to the McMartin lawsuit file. It also so happened, I later learned, that Mrs. Smith had herself been molested as a child when she was the same age as Christine was now. She read the Mc Martin lawsuit, and she could not help herself from internalizing the trauma. It became such an underlying emotional problem to her that she began crying and worrying about Christine, who had Mr. Lieberman as her teacher in our school. Now Mr. Lieberman, Mr. Norm, as the students called him, was the favorite teacher of all the students and their parents in either of our schools. He was so popular that every parent insisted that their child be assigned to his class. Not only did he teach kindergartners to read fluently in just a few weeks, they would also excel in writing, math, social studies, music, science, physical education, and drama under his tutelage. He was also the school choral director and, additionally, the drama club director who assisted children in presenting the most magnificent productions our school had ever seen. His class became too large because of popular demand from the parents, so I specifically designed his class so he would have a full-time teaching assistant as well as one or two parent volunteers to assist with the larger class size.

The name of our elementary school at that time was McKinney School. A book I had recently published, *The Song of Sounds*, was quite well-known in public education; and in the legislature, my name was easily recognized as one who stood for the highest in educational excellence. Our schools became incorporated in 1981. It was very easy for Mrs. Smith to take her copy of the McMartin lawsuit and change *McMartin* to *McKinney* and file the same lawsuit against our school. The day that lawsuit hit the front page of the *Press-Telegram*, it seemed that the sky was falling.

I had finally taken a much-needed vacation to the Caribbean Islands for a scuba diving trip. Trying to assist my employees to become self-reliant, I had advised them to try to solve their problems the best that they could and that I would not be taking any calls during that week of vacation. I had never given that advice before or after that time. Arriving home after that vacation, my first telephone call was from *Lieutenant Colonel Anderson, who was the parent of *Mary, a kindergarten child in our school. He said he wanted to go to my home immediately. He came in and sat on the front couch and blurted out, "Did you know that Mr. Norm molested Mary during class time? He molested her while he was teaching her to read. He molested her while he was directing the choral group. What are you going to do about it?" My shock was instant. This could not be possible. Why, he teaches in an open classroom which has no doors, he has an assistant teacher, and his desk is in full visibility of the office and the school director's desk. There would be no place for him to hide. Maybe if he had told me that Mr. Norm took Mary to the annex or into the restroom or somewhere in privacy, I could have contemplated the possibility, but to molest her during reading in front of everyone? Mr. Norm always sat or leaned against a table while directing the choral group of fifty students with three other teachers always present; how could he molest a child at the same time? I was told then that the police had come to the school, handcuffed Mr. Norm in front of the kindergarten class, and placed him in the Long Beach City Jail. He was being held on $50,000 bail. Now Mr. Norm was a quiet Jewish man, about thirty-five years of age, with curly red hair, a ball-game enthusiast, and an ardent golfer in his spare time. He was engaged to and living with Jean Hammer,* his fiancée, whose daughter Betty* was also in his kindergarten class. I couldn't imagine that Mr. Norm could or would jeopardize his reputation or the reputation of our school and stoop to touch any child inappropriately. After all my previous familiarity concerning molestations which happened in the public schools, I could not believe it was possible to happen in this open-space kindergarten class in a small private school. I had implicitly warned all my teachers to never ever touch a child. I had recently been appointed to the governor's committee on child molestation because of my reputation and being able to understand and prevent such incidents. All that I could think of was that since I warned my teachers to never touch a child, possibly if Mr. Norm had placed his arm on the shoulder of a child while reading or directing the choral group and that the child might have said "Mr. Norm touched me," the parent then might have jumped to the conclusion that Mr. Norm had sexually molested their child.

Decisions had to be made immediately. The first question was whether or not to raise bail in order for Mr. Norm to be released from jail. Number two was which attorney to hire to represent me. Number three would be to arrange for a substitute teacher in the kindergarten class, and on and on the crises grew. The most unbelievable escalation of events erupted. I received a threatening call from a man who claimed that he was in the governor's office in Sacramento; but he refused to identify himself, threatening that if I didn't resign from my governor-appointed position within one hour, they were there to threaten the governor. Hindsight would tell me that I should have called my attorney and fought hard against this threat; however, I certainly did not want my problems to spill over into the governor's office. I considered the governor to be a friend even though we were only on last-name speaking terms, but nonetheless, I didn't want him personally dragged into my impending lawsuit. Under pressure and after thinking it over for almost an hour, I called the secretary to the governor and offered my resignation. I had enjoyed my first committee meeting and felt that I had a lot to offer on that committee, which would be valuable for the future of children in California; therefore, I felt a deep disappointment that I had been forced into resigning.

Troubles piled upon troubles as I sought to keep the school operating in exemplary condition and finances in order and still squeeze enough time to attend all but one deposition of the eight or nine children who jumped on the lawsuit wagon. The only deposition that I missed was one held in Scotland, where Lieutenant Colonel Anderson* was stationed with his family. By now he had already added Mary's younger sister, Alicia*, who came up with a similar story. According to the transcript, Mary also added that Mr. Lieberman had placed a slimy substance into her hand while she was reading aloud to him at his desk while the other children were resting their heads on their desks. After being the person responsible for the extensive court costs of flying my attorneys first class to Scotland and other destinations, I was still determined to win this fight. The reporters from the *Press-Telegram* followed me to meetings which I held in a nearby public-school auditorium in which I made explanations as to what was happening. I was misquoted in the morning papers, misrepresented, and maligned in the news media. Many of the parents, who had loved and supported Mr. Lieberman, were now meeting in clusters before and after school and were threatening to burn the school. I actually had to read the newspaper each morning to determine if it would be safe for me to enter the school grounds. Unbelievably, according to the depositions and the news media, I was being charged as a coconspirator who, as in the McMartin lawsuit allegations, had conspired to arrange for molestation to thrive within my classrooms. Now that I was personally the target of the lawsuit, it became clear to me and my attorneys that the suing parents were after deep pockets, in other words, this was a great opportunity for them to make money.

The insurance company representing me and paying for portions of my expenses were also having their own problems within the state of California. Later I was to learn that funds would be withheld from insurance companies in California unless they had reached a certain level of loss during that current year; therefore, one minute prior to midnight on December 31, 1987, my insurance company settled these lawsuits for a million dollars per child, thus ensuring that the insurance company would be receiving future funds from the state of California for the coming year. The case had not even been finished, nor had I been consulted. There is no way we would have lost this molestation case had the entire cross-examining been completed. I would never have advised the insurance company to jump the gun and dole out a million dollars to each child (held in trust until their eighteenth birthday) for the many concocted stories which they told. There were many witnesses who should also have been called to the stand and been deposed. After all, these were not murder cases or even rape. Since when, if any thread were even remotely true, should children be awarded a million dollars for such stories of fantasy and at my expense? Had they been injured? The children were not the ones upset, but the parents who were following the details of the

Mc Martin case were visibly shaken, often crying on the stand and very emotionally involved.

Later I learned that nearly every mother involved in the lawsuit had herself been sexually molested at a very young age. They wept on the witness stand as they obviously relived the pain of their own childhood molestation experiences. They had each one dutifully questioned their daughters time and time again, receiving "no" answers. Pressing harder and harder and finally to their searching satisfaction, almost every daughter said "Yes, he touched me while he was directing the school chorus, during reading, or while he was directing the school play."

Now it so happened that a certain politician was running for office in our area, and what better platform to run on than that of "cleaning up Long Beach"! They were off and running, and we were to spend every last dime we had in order to protect our reputation and ultimately save our schools for the hundreds of students and their families who really wanted a good education for their child. A full book could be written about each girl named in the lawsuit and the reasons why each girl and her respective parents fell into this scam. The only two depositions which I did not personally attend were the daughter and her sister who were the children of the lieutenant colonel. He had been transferred to Scotland by the time of their depositions, and both their attorney and my insurance appointed attorney happily flew off to Scotland for a week's vacation in order to depose those two girls. Yes, I read the transcript of those dispositions and found their words even harder to believe. Children don't deliberately lie; however, they can be very quick to try to please their parents and "go along with the program."

Rather than finish the legal case against me, my corporation, and my schools, the insurance company took advantage of a limited timeline in which insurance companies had to report their losses for that year in order to be in a certain category for funding for the next year. Therefore, at 11:59 p.m. on December 31, 1987, my insurance company settled this case and turned in their probably twenty-million-dollar loss for this case. Nine girls have, by now, reached their eighteenth birthdays and have already been awarded a million dollars each for their participation in the hoax. Even if the wildest accusations of being touched while their teacher was sitting on the table and directing the drama club or fondling while he was teaching reading in front of the class and in front of other teachers, were found to be true, it should have been considered a minimum crime as opposed to rape, kidnapping and murder. In as much as there was never a witness supporting the allegations and all witnesses believed that nothing ever happened, it is hard for me to believe that this was other than a highly concocted political maneuver.

Regarding the teacher, he pled guilty in a plea bargain that allowed him to live in the city of Minneapolis and be gainfully employed there in a different occupation with the condition that he attends weekly therapy sessions. He was forbidden to ever teach or be with children again. If he was innocent as I still contend, our legal system was shortsighted, and students lost an award-winning teacher of which there are few and far between. If he was guilty of somehow sneaking in and fondling those five-year-old girls, then I think he should have had a greater sentence. Additionally, no girl ever said that he molested her in a private corner or away from other children or adults. The fact that the children all said that he molested them in front of the class while he was actively teaching made me believe that those families did not understand what molestation meant, and perhaps they thought it meant that if he rested his hand on their shoulder, that might suggest molestation. I'm sure that we will never know.

Regarding the McMartin molestation case, after a full year of investigations and a lengthy trial, the case was thrown out. The McMartin family was proven innocent, but unfortunately they were never able to pick up the pieces and put their school back together again.

CHAPTER 26

CHAIRMAN OF TWO BANK BOARDS

Simultaneously with the stressful years of litigation at the schools, I had been invited to become a charter board member of a new bank that was forming in Orange County. This was of great interest and a wonderful challenge for me. This bank, which was named New City Bank, was granted a charter and given the additional focus to include religious and church-related businesses as their clients. This was the first bank in the state of California to be allowed to officially serve religious organizations. The president of the bank, Wallace Linn, had been the president of National Bank in Long Beach, which had been serving the banking needs of my school business even when my parents owned the school. He was impressed with the growth of my schools, my business sense, and my political reputation. I gave a lot of consideration as to whether this was the exact bank that I would want to be associated with, but after several interviews with other board members and after being accepted by them, I decided to become an investor and an active board member. The board, however, had their own reservations about accepting me into their board. The biggest problem in their judgment appeared to be the fact that I was a single divorced woman. That judgmental attitude was a definite red flag to me, but I felt secure enough in my own worthiness and self-esteem to be able to hold my own as the only woman on an eleven-member board. As it turned out, I was most often outvoted by a ten-to-one vote. It was of some comfort that as least two other board members were of the same philosophy as I was, and frequently, they voted in the same way as I did.

I was active on the automobile-leasing company which our bank owned. I was not on the loan committee, and by the time the loan-committee minutes were brought before the full board, I was outvoted or ignored regarding my reluctance in honoring certain loans. In one specific case, I had warned the board regarding a $675,000 loan which was being granted to a gentleman who was starting a sports casting television show. I had already been approached by this same person for a personal loan for the same purpose, but I believed that he would not be able to keep his commitment to repay this loan. I was right, and his loan became an overdraft, which was unfortunate for the bank.

The New City Bank in Orange grew in assets and reputation. I was on the committee which sponsored a large golf tournament at the Industry Hills Golf Course in Industry Hills. Many celebrities joined our bank, and we were granted an expansion for a second bank in the city of Anaheim, in the new redevelopment center of the city. This second bank also did very well but had a little more difficulty attracting clients in the redevelopment part of that city. We believed that as the development process of the city would near its completion, we would also be very strong there.

This was during the time in 1987 when interest rates were escalating to 15 percent, then 19 percent and finally up to 22 percent. It was a very difficult time for banks. Interestingly enough, people were coming from Australia and New Zealand to try to arrange loans to refinance apartment complexes and other commercial properties there. The interest rates in those countries were exceeding 44 percent, and the possibility of refinancing at even 22 percent looked very attractive to them. We did not fund any loans to those people, but I became friends with several and later visited them and enjoyed an inside look into their countries. Actually, I was invited to be a guest on a radio talk show in New Zealand, which is a whole other story.

Many banks began failing, but there was never a hint of a problem within our banks until one day when the Federal Deposit Insurance Company (commonly known as FDIC) inspectors arrived and flagged several loans which they considered to have problems. We were able to clean up those problems and were praised by FDIC for having such a strong bank. They, in fact, awarded our bank a high rating and authorized the sale of additional stock in January of 1986. However, soon after that sale of stock was completed, FDIC representatives entered our bank on a Friday evening in March of 1986, locked the doors, confiscated the bank, and held a secret (prearranged) auction sale of the bank after closing hours that same night. Our two banks were sold for $325,000, and all assets amounting to nearly twenty-five million were seized by the FDIC.

Two weeks prior to the seizure, FDIC had secretly identified a number of loans which they again stated had problems. They said that they would allow our bank to continue if we would purchase those identified loans for one and a half million dollars. After a board meeting, I met with two other board members and told them that I could raise the money within twenty-four hours if they would like to become partners and share in the loan package. We studied the list of loans which totaled four and a half million dollars in loan value and then agreed to make the purchase. The next decision had to do with whether we would retain the collection process collectively or to divide the loan package and each partner collects his or her loans separately. The two other partners were Herb Leo, who was one of the early founding board members, and Duane Logsdon, who was accepted as a board member even later in the process than I had been accepted. Herb Leo was a staunch Christian businessman who was the owner of a large food company and was heavily involved on the committee that was working for the city of Anaheim redevelopment project. It was his uppermost interest to eradicate the poverty and slum areas of Anaheim and develop a beautiful new center to the city of Anaheim. It was his dream that a bank that could respectfully serve the religious community was also of paramount value in the professional and highly attractive new city center of Anaheim. He was also on the board for the Anaheim Memorial Hospital and was actively pursuing the latest in medical equipment for a truly state-of-the-art medical center. He had invited me several times to tour the medical facility and to see for myself the latest acquisitions of medical equipment which he had been instrumental in securing for the hospital. Unfortunately, I never found or made time to accept his invitations; however, he continually kept me informed on their progress. During his tenure as a board member, I recall that he himself was treated at the Anaheim Memorial Hospital with angioplasty in order to open up clogged arteries in his heart. After his treatment, his health seemed miraculously improved, and in his early seventies he continued working long hours on behalf of the bank as well as his continued position as chief executive officer for the large food company which he owned. Leo again invested over two hundred thousand dollars in the purchase of stock for New City Bank only two weeks prior to the FDIC takeover. You see, FDIC had complimented our bank board for making a recovery after we purchased that loan package, authorized our bank to expand and sell more stock, and advised us to add more new board members and continue our exemplary banking business. Leo made some headway with his portion of the loan collections. He decided to move his whole family to Prescott, Arizona, but he died suddenly of a massive heart attack soon after he moved there. He was followed in death by his wife later in the same week. I believe that the loss of probably over a million dollars in the FDIC confiscation of New City Bank was most likely the overwhelming trauma which caused both of their deaths.

Duane Logsdon, in his late sixties, had retired some years prior to investing in New City Bank from a large business which he owned. He also had spent approximately twenty years in ministering alongside Hermano Pablo, a traveling evangelist. He managed their programming, musical productions, and finances. He had been invited to become a board member and an investor of New City Bank due to his high visibility in the Christian community. He gave considerable thought and prayer before he made his decision to become a board member. This was a pattern of each and every board member. Not only had each board member become successful in the business world, but each one was also willing to share his talents in order to make this bank the most successful bank in California. Duane's original investment of $225,000, he believed, would be a wise investment and his knowledge and wisdom could surely be of great benefit to this bank board. He, as well as every other board member, had fully committed personally as well as financially to this banking endeavor; and each member took their positions seriously. Board meetings were opened with a prayer that every decision would be guided and blest by our Heavenly Father. I well remember that during the last fifteen minutes of one very long evening board meeting, as I glanced across the table, I noted that Duane's color in his face changed from a healthy ruddy complexion to an off-color pallor with shades of yellow or gray. I watched him a moment and believed that he probably was suffering the onset of an illness. I don't at this time recall the motions that were so crucial as to keep us in a meeting until after 9:00 p.m.; but immediately after the meeting when Duane's wife, Carol, arrived to meet him, I made my way over to speak with her. "Carol," I said, "I don't want to alarm you, but I noticed that Duane's color in his face changed at one point in the last few minutes of our board meeting. I would suggest that you to take him to the doctor as soon as possible for a physical." It turned out that Duane had suffered adrenal gland failure and could have died within days without immediate treatment. He did return to normal health and was healthy at the time we purchased the FDIC loan package. Notwithstanding that fact, less than two years later and prior to completing his loan collections, he suffered a massive brain tumor, had brain surgery but gradually regained some semblance of normalcy. He later passed away from many complications from that brain surgery.

At the time of the FDIC bank loan purchase which the three of us made, I was appointed as the new bank chairman with new duties which commanded my undivided attention and which became my highest priority. I met the challenge with some humility, acknowledging to myself that the eight or so board members who had continually outvoted me needed now to be convinced of my leadership and the survivorship of our bank. The first and most difficult task at hand was to terminate the services of the president, Wally Linn, who had given his whole life's energy and determination toward developing a "glorious" bank which had begun to appear to be much to his own self-adulation. He was polished and wanted everything to be the best. He went so far as to represent himself and this bank to the federal government on television with celebrities and church pastors and their audiences. He was on a roll, and this bank had seemed to provide his ticket to stardom. Now after resisting my counsel regarding many issues in which he smirked in a board meeting, saying, "What must we do around here in order to make Phyllis happy?" I was the one who had been right in nearly every instance; and had he ever heeded the business sense which I exhibited, we might never have come to the day in which the board voted for me to be the chairman and the person appointed to personally dismiss him.

The private meeting I called with Wally Linn was very somber, straightforward, and firm. I explained the board had taken action to bring about his dismissal and that I wanted to thank him for his efforts. I also explained that the board had voted to initiate a different approach toward the management of the bank. He argued that I couldn't do that to him . . . I simply couldn't do that to him. What would he do with his life now? How could this be? Wouldn't I argue on his behalf in order to change the mind of the board? With calm gentleness and reserve, I assured him that the decision was final, and I hoped the best for him and his family in the future.

CHAPTER 27

LATENT BUSINESS SENSE AWAKENED

I felt a great compulsion and urgency to get involved in some kind of a venture which would be more challenging and yet personally fulfilling for me. The school business was difficult and time-consuming, and attacks on me were painful. Never in my wildest dreams would I have suspected that a political undercurrent could undermine my efforts and intentions in providing an exemplary, loving educational environment for children. It was especially hurtful, considering that this was not even my first choice for a career. I had originally desired to become a medical research scientist, and I still believed that was my highest calling in life. Finances and family pressure turned me on a path toward public and later private education.

One day when driving with a friend I noticed a large forlorn house which was less than one-fourth completed and which had stood abandoned through weather and storms for more than four years. It was a 6,100-square-foot estate home on an acre parcel in the elite Indian Springs area of Chatsworth, California. I was so taken with this abandoned project that the next time I saw it, I asked to stop and walk through the rubble of unfinished carpentry, piles of dirt, debris, and puddles of mud and stagnant water everywhere. This was it! I knew it immediately! There was just something about the project, the air, distant ocean breeze, the sunshine, and the nearness to the mountains which drew me to want to complete this project. I believed that I could finish the project and turn it into something beautiful. It was an enormous undertaking with no promise of success.

First I needed to purchase the property, so I immediately placed a bid, which was accepted. Then a foreman would be needed who could assist with coordinating on-site contractors. I would oversee the total project; make all the decisions; and as soon as the roof, doors, and windows were finished, I moved a bed in and lived there while the building projects were ongoing.

Meantime, I commuted daily over fifty miles each way, overseeing the school program and continuing with the fallout from the banking fiasco as well as the new collection process for the bad loan package which the three of us had purchased. We had by now dissolved our banking partnership and divided the loan package into three equal packages. Also, the renovation of the three ranches I owned in the Fallbrook area was still in progress. They needed as much attention as I could give them on the weekends. I still was involved in a partnership with Gildner and Shanks Company for the construction of twenty-six homes which were to be built in the Fontana area.

Life was extremely busy time at this time for me. It had been nearly twenty years since my divorce from my children's father and also a second brief failed marriage soon after that first divorce. Certainly by this time I had had enough of failed relationships which usually seemed to simply bring more frustration into my life. This was a time to enjoy my businesses and use my creativity.

The development of the Chatsworth property consumed nearly all my attention but turned out to be one of the most satisfying things I had ever done in my life. It was a place of serene beauty and tranquility. It withstood the 1992 earthquake with only a fingernail-size chip in one of the marble fireplaces. My carpenters placed extra studs and steel straps between the joists throughout. Even though the carpenters complained, stating that this house did not need to be built any stronger than the general building code requires, I persisted in wanting it to be built strong enough to withstand a big earthquake. When the earthquake hit, I was on a skiing trip in Colorado. There was no telephone communication to the Chatsworth area for hours, and I waited impatiently as TV and radio announcers described the devastation in that whole area. There were many deaths being reported from apartment buildings that collapsed. There was fortunately no destruction to my property, which was empty at the time.

The next day, I spoke with my foreman, who told me of ten or eleven homes surrounding my house that were flattened during the earthquake. He agreed that there had not been any damage to my house. Prior to my ski trip, I had listed the Chatsworth house with a real estate broker, and an offer was being drawn up from a contractor from Texas the very night before the quake. Unfortunately, due to the devastation surrounding my property, the pending offer was cancelled. That sale would have provided a sizable profit for my three years' work in developing that property. Due to the earthquake, it would take another two to three years for anyone to even consider purchasing property in that area again. Finally, the owner of the El Presidente restaurants purchased the property from me at a bargain price for him. I was able to recover all my building expenses; but in hindsight, if I had held the property for one more year, I would have received the profits which I truly deserved for such a distinguished home in that area. Nonetheless, Mr. Ruffinilli and his wife truly loved their new home. They even purchased my Chinese silk carpets and proudly showed off their home to me after they completed furnishing it. This house could easily have been featured in *Better Homes and Gardens*. Mr. Ruffinilli added commercial decorative concrete patio furniture, a trellis patio roof, an additional commercial barbeque, fruit orchards, and several herb gardens to supply special spices for their restaurants. I had originally had the whole acre professionally landscaped with lawns adjacent to the pool and spa area as well as a private golfing green. The new owners were not the least bit interested in the golfing area; so they immediately converted that area to a play yard for their grandchildren, which seemed a little out of character for the property but became a happy place for their grandchildren, I'm sure. This one-of-a-kind home was, I believe, truly amazing.

CHAPTER 28

POWER OF OPPOSITION

It took awhile for me to recognize the power of political savvy. To be sure, the opposite of good is evil. If evil is to overtake good, it must become more powerful; and in order to become more powerful, it must connive ways to look more attractive or else make something or someone look bad. I have had experiences with many different forms of evil trying to squelch good or righteousness, and I will describe a few situations where this seems to be the case.

Previously, I described how one mother deceived her attorney boss and changed the name in one lawsuit to my name and ran the same lawsuit against my business, my employees, my family, and myself.

Another case involved leadership of a statewide organization, in which the opposition group wanted the power to become the new leaders. In order to bring about such a strategy, they took a statement which I had previously made, took it out of context, and projected it as a fact whereas their concocted statement made it appear as a complete lie. This became a false accusation; however, when people spread rumors with a malicious purpose in mind, such as an attempt to win the power they seek, it is difficult to disprove their claims. The supposed tarnish on a person's reputation, if the public can be coerced into believing someone is a liar, is a sure killer when running for office.

The case where I was appointed by the governor to be a representative on a state committee appeared so dangerous politically to the opponents who were intent on winning their own political race that they smeared my reputation, threatened me, and additionally threatened to ruin my reputation with the governor if I would not resign within an hour from my appointment. It was so totally unexpected that I did not seek legal representation but resigned in order to avoid further threats. Not only did I resign from that committee, but I also resigned from each of my other posts in other statewide organizations. Perhaps that was the chicken thing to do, but I only have so much energy to give; and if the opposition was becoming too powerful, I retreated to seek a calmer place in life.

I am truly thankful that President Bush did not back down when threatened and called names when the opposition tried to smear and ruin his reputation. He stood firm in spite of booing and negative criticism. The stakes are high, and the road is rough for those trying to lead and do the right thing. This seems to be true all through life. Perhaps the only thing that will insulate a person from such negative opposition is the faith and strength which one receives upon placing their trust in Jesus as their savior.

The same issues are prevalent in the world today. Terrorism seems to be the underlying hidden foundation in certain radical extremist religions. It is my understanding that it is their stated intent to kill anyone who does not believe as they believe. Could they connive, deceive and devise plans to overtake freedom and democracy in the world even if other people do not believe as they want them to believe? A similar principle is at work within our own two party democratic systems. Leaders in the defeated party usually oppose or are against anything the winning party stands for. For example one party seems to hate the mere mention of the words "In God we trust". They fought and argued to get God and prayer out of the public schools; however, after winning their leaders seem to turn around and meekly mimic the words, "God bless America", in order to appease the losing party. They try to prove outwardly that they really are the good party. *They appear to be wolves in sheep clothing, so to speak. They are hoping that those who hold the* opposing views will become confused and fall into line with the current administration and hopefully change their opinion and vote for them instead at the next election.

Every man, woman and child needs to understand the basic principles of good versus evil. Without a foundation based on Biblical principles, it might be difficult to decipher evil intentions when they seem to be cloaked in nice intentions, good clothing, education, news media, etc. The watchful person will soon learn to tell the difference and the sooner the better for each of us.

CHAPTER 29

FDIC ATTACK

No sooner had three of us on the board of directors purchased the loan package, which comprised every loan that the Federal Deposit Insurance Company inspectors tagged as possibly having an irregularity, than the FDIC regulators began changing their minds. I had made sure that in purchasing the loan package for over one million dollars, there would be greater value in equity within those loans when collected. Perhaps the inspectors had not taken the equity factor into consideration when they tagged those loans. One particular loan which became my personal property when the loans were divided was what I called the Lincoln automobile property. Before I even knew what was happening, the FDIC had taken out a lawsuit against me personally for the Lincoln automotive property, which they claimed belonged to them. One can hardly realize the intimidation techniques which I was to encounter in the months to come as I literally fought for my reputation and my legal rights. The initial court hearing was only the first of their intimidation tricks. I had hired an attorney, who happened to be an acquaintance of mine, to represent me in our first hearing. I was ushered into a large conference room and asked to sit at the center of a long conference table. Immediately, my attorney, who thought this hearing was anything but serious, was asked to sit at the end of the conference table. He seemed to be unforgivably naive in that he wore a white t-shirt with large red letters which read, "My Attorney Can Beat Up Your Attorney." It was only a brief minute until the conference doors opened and in marched six FDIC attorneys all dressed in black suits, white shirts, and black ties. My embarrassment was overshadowed by the fact that the procedures for that hearing were meant to cause me to believe that I had somehow stolen an FDIC property, and they were going to claim it no matter what I said or did.

Eventually, I found it necessary to hire two other new attorneys to represent me. I won that case against the FDIC; sold the property for $750,000; and along with another mountain home property which I sold, easily regained my purchase price for the loan package as well as recovered my loss in my original bank investment. My pride and self-worth were bruised again, but I got up and moved on immediately into more and different kinds of business ventures.

CHAPTER 30

DESIGNING YOUR OWN THERAPY

It is important to understand one's own talents, personality, energy level, health and financial assets in this life. Boys and girls should be encouraged when they are very young to learn about themselves including their talents and unique personality and their responsibilities in life. They need to learn that they are in charge of their own destiny and they can be anything they want to be when they grow up. Possibilities are unlimited. Generally children who have everything done for them and have everything given to them do not develop the ability to think for themselves. They grow up continuing to be dependent upon their parents to support them, pay for their college education, buy a car for them and so forth. Since they did not learn to take responsibility for their own life, they are more susceptible to believing the government should take care of them the same way their parents did. They believe the government should provide all kinds of programs, food stamps, medical insurance, funds for housing, college tuition and scholarships, etc. Rarely would a child who has been taught that he can learn to make money in many different ways doing the things that he is best at in life, ever need or want help from the government. Taking responsibility for one's own welfare is a very entrepreneurial attitude in life. These people are the ones who create their own livelihood; hire workers to promote their creative ideas, set up successful businesses and who usually become wealthy due to their work ethics and attitude toward life and supporting others.

Early in childhood and at young ages, my children were inventing ways to earn their own money. They enjoyed saving all their money and using it to further some of their investment ideas. Some of their ideas are worthy of mention.

Beginning at about age five, each of my children was personally involved in saving their money. They had discovered that every penny counts and that a penny saved is the same as a penny earned. There were countless ways of adding to their savings. One way was to help with extra jobs, whether it was a special project for Grandpa, the next-door neighbor, or even for Mom. Another way was, as I mentioned before, to begin salvaging parts that were being discarded at a nearby bicycle shop or even finding old bikes set out for trash collection and refurbishing them for a quick sale. Somehow or other, my two sons, Curtis and David, learned how to assemble all the discarded bicycle parts and then they were able to build a bicycle which looked brand-new out of those used parts. Rarely did they have to purchase any additional parts in order to complete a bicycle that looked new enough to sell. The newly built bicycle would be painted, the chrome polished and a sign placed on it making it available for anyone interested in purchasing it. The bicycles sold for $60 to $100 each, and the boys instinctively enjoyed the fruits of a sprouting new business adventure. That special gift of the bicycle they built for their grandfather for Christmas did far more for their self-images and for his opinion of their abilities than anything else they could have given him. Their grandfather was so surprised and proud of their accomplishment that he jumped on the bike and began riding down the street.

Later on, their projects became larger and larger, sometimes causing me to want to second-guess the outcome. One such project was to paint the entire outside of our house. The boys were still quite young, about ten and fifteen. The motivation for painting the house was to change the color. The house had been pink when I purchased it, and unbeknownst to me, this color was an embarrassment to them. David commented that he didn't like telling his friends that he lived in the pink house. At any rate, I finally agreed; and weeks later, our house was sparkling white with dark charcoal-blue trim. It looked stunningly handsome and obviously very stately in comparison to the pink color which I had merely accepted and taken for granted. I was pleased with the outcome, and I surprised each of the boys by handing them a $100 bill as my extra little thank-you to them.

My children never received an allowance. They were told that we were all in this together as a family and we could extend our money by saving and investing it or we could waste our money and never be able to buy what was really important to us or something very special. That something special had been our first new house which had a lovely swimming pool and provided for many hours of fun for our family and our friends. Prior to buying that house, we had lived in one rented house after another, barely making ends meet each month. After the divorce from their father, we determined as a family to begin a very strict savings program, and it worked. Within three years, we had selected a house within walking distance and central to all their activities including their schools, public library, church, and gymnastic and piano lessons. I had been driving the children to each of their activities many times each week; and since I was working two jobs, attending college part-time, picking up their babysitter, etc., I sometimes felt more like a taxi driver than a mother. Finding a place within walking distance was so important to me that I literally sat down with a map and drew a circle around all the places that I had to drive to each week. Then for three years, instead of waiting in the car while they took their lessons, I drove up and down all the streets within that circle until I found a small house that might work.

The real estate lady was very clever in that she invited my children, who were then seven, ten, and twelve, to swim in the pool while I was inspecting the house. That gesture made a lot of points with the children, but now I would have to make a decision and select one of the houses I was considering, which wasn't easy. No banker would lend money in that era to a divorced woman. It simply wasn't done. Therefore, when my offer was written up, I discovered that the banks had been notified that I was a widow. This was an effort on the part of the real estate broker to protect me and assure me of receiving a loan. My loan would have been denied based solely on my divorce status. When I found out about that disclosure, I refused to go forward with the purchase until the truth was told. I had a secure teaching position with the public schools, and I believed that I was totally responsible and did not want someone bending the truth or lying on my behalf. As it turned out, the sellers were interested in carrying the note for my purchase. I was interested in receiving the lowest interest rate possible, and I found that if I placed a $5,000 down payment instead of only $3,000, the interest rate would drop from 5 ½ percent to 4 ¾ percent. This seemed worth going after, and I thought that I might request a three-year loan from my father in just this one instance. Lending money was not something that was ever done in my family. I was expected to always manage my own financial affairs.

During the utterly unbelievable poverty times in my marriage, when there was literally no money for food and I was pregnant and would have to take a job in order to buy food for the family, I was never given a single dollar. It was therefore a gigantic step that I was taking to approach my father in order to request a three-year loan of $5,000 for the down payment to buy this house. It so happened that my mother had made a trip to Iowa to visit her mother, my grandmother, during that period. Since she was away, perhaps my father had a soft spot in his heart, took advantage of the situation, and agreed to make the loan to me. The whole idea of this loan was not well received when my mother returned and found out about it. Nonetheless, the house was finally in escrow at the price of $27,500. Monthly payments were to be $135.47 per month for the next fifteen years, and payments on the loan to my father would be $145.85 for three years. Happily, I met all these payments plus the ongoing expenses of the home, the private lessons, and oh yes, the many medical bills which the children kept incurring. It is true that I received $60 per month for each of our three children until they reached eighteen; however, that never began to cover even 50 percent of their expenses. Now, however, I was meeting a new problem. The escrow was nearly ready to close, but my constantly contested five year divorce proceedings had not been finalized. This would ultimately cause a greater problem unless I could get their father to sign a quitclaim deed on the house. I was not sure that this would be possible, but when he found out that he might become responsible for the payments if he did not sign off, he readily signed the quitclaim deed.

Buying and decorating our new home became the first of many new projects which were like special therapy for me. The next large project which I declared as my ongoing therapy was the purchase of a ten-acre parcel of ranchland in San Diego County. This property had belonged to my parents and acreage had been the love of his life for my father. Unusual and unique as it was, it also had a complexity of problems within its perimeter. Shortly after my father passed away in February of 1978, a one-hundred-year flood engulfed that ranchland. The beautiful little stream which flowed year round through the center of the property became a raging 1,500-foot-wide torrential river, taking with it everything in sight. That meant that the beautiful white horse-corral fencing was gone, my father's boat and boat trailer were gone, the lovely lake where my father fished for trout every morning he stayed on the ranch filled in with silt and sand, and every hint of the lake completely vanished from the property. The job of caring for this ranchland became a great burden for my mother; and in her frustration, she threatened that if I did not care for the property, she would make arrangements to donate the property to a gentleman who flew in from Texas to receive and record her donation. She called me to witness the transaction, but I smelled foul play and called his bluff upon which he left quickly without even saying good-bye to her. Soon thereafter, I managed to offer to purchase the ranchland for $110,000 plus the gift of a new Buick for my mother. She accepted this and was happy with her car and also relieved of the problems with the ranch.

The ranch took on an entirely different character when I arrived to begin cleaning it up. When the raging floods and river went through the property in 1978, it had carried and dropped thousands of willow seeds from wooded areas upstream, and these willow trees took root and grew rapidly on every square foot of the property. They were already up to ten or fifteen feet tall in just the three or four years which had passed. My therapy program was about to begin. First I would need a tractor strong enough to clear the land. I ventured into the Fallbrook Tractor Store and decided to purchase a new 30 hp Kubota diesel tractor with a front loader, a disk, and a rake. This would mean that I would not be able to purchase the new car I felt I needed, but instead I would put more than 195,000 miles on my Toyota Supra and purchase the new tractor instead.

I discovered that I could use the front loader to push over the willow trees one tree at a time. It was long and hard work, but I stuck to it and eventually made contact with the Regional Occupational Program in nearby Oceanside at the high school and requested to train high school students in working on a ranch. Those students were great. Five high school students joined my project; and with their help and that of another friend, we built an "outhouse," a tool shed, fencing, installed an irrigation system, planted pumpkins, learned to drive the tractor, dug up tree stumps, cleared brush, and held a controlled-burn day with the fire department supervising the controlled fire. Additionally, there were day laborers who wanted extra jobs, and I found many of them very helpful as we began to create a beautiful ranch again. No one could ever visualize how beautiful the ranch had been at one time, nor could they imagine a lake with my father fishing for trout from his boat every day. One problem remained and that being that there was no house or buildings on the ten-acre property. I plotted and planned to build a home on the hillside, but the costs seemed prohibitive. A new bridge would have to be built, and a road carved into the hillside would be very expensive. Also, the planning department was discouraging any building in that area due to the new designation of that area being declared a flood zone.

One morning when I was working at our school in Long Beach, I received a call from Gloria, who was a real estate agent and a longtime friend of our family. She had known about my ranch in Fallbrook, and she wanted to know if I might be interested in a foreclosure she had just heard about which was also in the Fallbrook area. I said that I probably wasn't interested, but if she would give me the address, I would drive there and look it over.

Immediately I called one of my banking friends, and we drove to Fallbrook, where we discovered a very picturesque 6.5-acre avocado ranch with a historic two-bedroom house and a cute guesthouse which had been built from a converted barn. There was also a beautiful little lake with its own fishing dock. The problem was that the property had been abandoned and had been severely burglarized with many thousands of dollars of visible destruction. The other problem was that there was only a twenty-four-hour period in which the foreclosure could be intercepted. I walked through the property quickly sizing up the problems. Two-thirds of the avocado trees were dead and the horse coral fencing appeared to be in complete disrepair. The guest house, which had been built to look like a converted barn was in complete shambles. There was evidence of illegal drugs and cans of paint strewn all over the carpets and brick flooring inside the home. There were evidence of illegal drugs and cans of paint strewn over the carpets and brick flooring in the house. I took a deep breath and said, "This would be too much of a problem for me to try to restore." That decision lasted throughout that day and until I slept on it overnight. Actually, I reasoned that purchasing this property with two houses already on it and an income-producing avocado grove would be less expensive in the long run than proceeding with trying to build a house on the other ten-acre parcel.

The next morning, I knew that I could make that property into a beautiful haven, and that meant that I needed to get into high gear and contact the gentleman who was being foreclosed upon to make an offer which would save him from foreclosure and perhaps give me a deal at the same time. This also meant that I would need to pay cash for his loan at his bank for about $150,000 as well as pay him $15,000 as an incentive and a cash settlement to him. All this worked perfectly. I met the deadline and now owned this second ranch, and at the same time, another brand-new therapy project was created.

This new ranch project would require more work than I had ever anticipated, but it was rewarding and very fulfilling. When it was completed, I was able to invite guests for wonderful retreats in the country. I had my trailer moved from the other ranch onto the top of the hill amongst the avocado orchard. When the converted barn, which was built and furnished as a guesthouse, was ready, I was able to sleep twelve guests overnight. Additionally, the guesthouse was soon rented to a lovely widowed lady who truly enjoyed living there.

As a member of a spiritual leader group from the Crystal Cathedral, we used this ranch as a weekend retreat center and found our work together very productive. During one retreat, it rained the whole time; however, the environment was so beautiful, quiet, and refreshing that no one even cared that it was raining. I loved cooking for large groups and was able to make the whole house feel like an exclusive restaurant. This again was a way of using talents in a way which was fun and very rewarding.

Another surprising reward came when we discovered that this latest six-acre ranch was the most fertile soil which we had ever seen and which we learned was the result of being one of the earliest horse ranches in that whole area. It was almost impossible with this rich soil to fail in the gardening and orchard department. We not only had fresh avocados;

but there were also ninety-eight pomegranate trees and several orange, lemon, peach, tangerine, walnut, and pecan trees bearing fruit abundantly. It was wonderful to gather fruit and vegetables for meals especially for frequent guests.

The horse corrals and chicken house provided places for goats and chickens which added fresh eggs to the menu. I had hoped for a horse while I was there, but that did not come about until many years later. My mother often commented that this would be the perfect place to live in the event of a disaster because a family could raise all of their own food and be self-sustaining.

Rosario, an elderly retired singer and guitar player from Mexico City, was soon hired. He lived in the little trailer at the top of the hill and cared for the property. He showed great ingenuity in gardening, planting, watering, and caring for the garden and all the fruit trees on the property. As a built-in benefit, he was always ready to entertain guests and receive a free meal at the same time. He didn't speak English, so it forced everyone else to improve on our Spanish-speaking skills. He was rather small in stature but very strong. He would work endless hours until he had everything looking meticulous. What a treat to drive up the long winding driveway, which was arched over with stately oak trees, and find the driveway swept, trees trimmed, trash emptied, lawn raked, and the garden growing profusely. He built trellises for the tomato and string bean plants. He made little irrigation trenches around every watermelon and pumpkin plant. He was able to grow tomatoes that were easily eight inches in diameter and huge watermelons that were deep red, crisp, and sweet. He was so enthusiastic and successful with his gardening that I gave him enough watermelon seeds to plant a full acre. The crop was beautiful; and we sold the watermelons to an organic grocery chain, which brought in a semi truck that maneuvered its way to the top of the hill in order to load several hundred of our beautiful watermelons. Additionally, I took many loads of the watermelon, filling the back of my Supra like a small pickup truck, to our schoolchildren for their special treats as well as to sell dozens and dozens to their parents. We always found ways to generate funds for special projects for our students.

These self-designed therapies were enjoyable even though each project required hours of robust physical effort. They were beautiful to enjoy and share with others as each new project was being transformed from a disaster situation into something attractive and also financially rewarding. This is probably the identical story for each of our school sites. It seems that each school site was at one time in deplorable condition; and then after purchasing it, with the help of many supporting workers, we transformed each property into something beautiful and educationally rewarding for hundreds of children. Perhaps I can see the same pattern with many of my employees. Often I hire a person who, I believe, has great potential but may not have finished their education and may even feel insecure about their ability to teach children; but after much training and guided experience, a successful employee emerges. It is truly rewarding to have a part in assisting another person in becoming successful as a teacher as well as watching each person get started on their road to financial success.

CHAPTER 31

SEARCHING THE WORLD FOR THE BEST EDUCATIONAL MODEL

Our private schools, which were incorporated in 1981, were 99 percent Caucasian when I first began directing them in 1975. Each succeeding year, we saw increasing color among our children and our families. After the riots of 1992, all Caucasian children, except for my own three grandchildren, left our schools due to their fear of the riot situation. It took yet another ten years for a balanced mixture of races to appear again. Children within our schools seem totally immune to race, color, or financial status of their families. Due to the multicultural population within our schools, I had determined to design our curriculum in order to bring our entire culturally diversified students to their highest potential and academic levels.

My experience teaching in the public schools of Iowa, Minnesota, and later in California taught me that there are great variations in educational models, curriculum framework, and styles of teaching. Test scores were beginning to decline very rapidly in the late seventies and the early eighties in the United States as compared with our counterparts in countries such as Asia, China, and Europe. I had to know what those differences were firsthand and find out quickly how we could upgrade our program to include any secrets of success which educators were enjoying in those countries. I would need to find a way to personally visit schools in each of those countries.

A mother of two of our students (a brother and a sister) became a travel agent. When I discussed my ambitious plan with her, she suggested that she would arrange and accompany me to Hong Kong and Taiwan. Two more friends joined this trip and accompanied me as I set about to investigate the public and private schools in those countries. A large public school in downtown Taipei was the first school I visited. It was a large two-story building built on all four sides of a city block surrounding a central playground. School began at 7:00 a.m. and continued until 5:00 p.m. with a one-hour break at noon. When the morning bell rang, the children, who were dressed in neatly starched and pressed uniforms, walked silently into their classrooms. The students sat, fifty to a room, in five rows of desks with ten children in each row. The children sat with perfect posture, both feet on the floor; and they listened intently while the teacher lectured, occasionally writing important information on the chalkboard for them to memorize or recite together. The students followed the lecture and information closely with references to their text book on each of their desks. Every student was on the same page. I learned that their school was in session from 7:00 a.m. to 5:00 p.m. from Monday through Friday as well as one or two evenings from 7:00 p.m. to 10:00 p.m. and also Saturday from 7:00 a.m. to 2:00 p.m. Obviously, those children were receiving nearly fifty-eight hours of classroom instruction each week in comparison to twenty for primary grades to possibly thirty hours per week for high school students in the United States. I observed that the instruction was very traditional with almost 100 percent of time in class comprised of lecture, memorizing facts, and working mathematical problems. I did not observe a single child who resisted listening to the teacher, showed a bad attitude, or even squabbled with another child. It was interesting to me years later to have several students sent to our school in Long Beach, California, from Taiwan for our ten-week summer session. Again, we experienced the same respect for learning and achievement from them as I had seen when they were in school in their homeland. Somehow, this respect for learning might be one of the secrets which I was searching for and which must have been taught to those children when they were very young and prior to attending school.

It was also of interest to me that during the one-hour break from school at noon, all of the 1,500 or more students went to the playground while their teachers locked their classroom doors until the bell rang for the students to once again file into their assigned seats with fifty students in each room. I noted immediately that there was no supervision on the playground, so I inquired of the principal as to why there was no adult supervision. I was told clearly that the school was not open during that period and the students would need to wait until the bell rang in order to return to school. When I questioned that situation again, I was told that it was not the responsibility of the teachers to supervise students when the school was closed for that hour. I noticed that there were children of all ages from five through probably twelve on the playground. Some of them walked by themselves to nearby neighborhood stores or restaurants to buy food while the school closed for that hour. I was struck by how much responsibility was entrusted to each student to care for himself during that period. The principal was shocked that I would even question the procedure of leaving approximately 1,500 to possibly up to 2,000 children together in a totally unstructured and unsupervised environment. But again, perhaps this might be a tiny portion of the secret to building pride, responsibility, and dedication in their children; and therefore they seemed to rise to the level of the high expectation and trust which was placed in each student.

The very next day, I visited a large private American school, also downtown in Taipei. I felt as if I had walked into my own school except that this was on a much grander scale. While touring the school, I noticed that these students had almost identical opportunities as the students in my own program. Then I learned that the principal had earned his teaching credentials from Iowa State Teachers College (now known as University of Northern Iowa) in Cedar Falls, Iowa, where I had also earned my early associate's degree in elementary teaching. We had designed our curriculum and the classrooms in the school in almost an identical manner. He had certainly presented in Taiwan an educational model which represented the very best that the United States has to offer. The educational teaching program at the University of Northern Iowa is second only to Columbia University in the United States. This American school presented a very open, flexible, and inviting feeling within this large, rambling school facility. Hallways which meandered from classroom to classroom were attractively lined with murals, artwork, sculptures, photo displays, beautiful live plants, and science exhibits.

Contrasting the American School in Taiwan with the public school system there were many striking differences which I might summarize as follows:

Traditional Taiwan Public School	Modern American School
—Structured	—Flexible
—Lecture-style teaching	—Experiential style of learning
—Rote memorization of facts	—Students and teachers involved learning together
—Lock-step schedule	—Flexible scheduling
—Military-style teaching	—Creativity encouraged
—No artistic expression	—Artistic expression
—One basic curriculum	—Flexible choice of subjects

Other countries and schools which I visited and studied were in China, Japan, Russia, and the Philippine Islands. Most of the schools which I visited seemed similar to the traditional Taiwan public school which I described earlier.

Additionally, the higher and more successful testing scores in those countries seemed to have to do with influences in the homes. Even in Taiwan, I observed very young children as well as school-age children sitting with their parents and working on their reading, math, and writing materials or even assigned schoolwork while with their parents in their place of business, behind the cash-register counter, or in a corner on the floor undistracted by busy shoppers. This turns out to be the third ingredient to successful test scores, and that is the seriousness with which parents involve their children at an early age. Obviously, the education of their children is given the highest priority by these parents. Children are taken to work with them, and the whole family helps in building a solid educational foundation as well as an attitude of urgency and high priority for learning. Overall, the time spent on learning in these more traditional countries is probably 75 percent of a child's waking hours; whereas, probably less than 10 to 20 percent of a child's waking hours in America would be spent on parent-directed influence and an urgency to learn and excel.

Observations in the Children's Palace in Beijing, China, indicated that children have a much greater capacity for skill development; exercising their talents; and learning complex musical, rhythmic, and dance skills than I would have formerly believed possible. Children in the age range of four through eight were playing a multitude of difficult musical instruments, reading the music, and participating as synchronized players in their symphonic orchestras. Other children were presenting advanced ballet performances for those of us who were visiting their classrooms. Never did I observe any child who showed reluctance toward the strict lessons, but instead, the children appeared extremely happy and tireless in their routines. I wondered how even this type of skill training could be integrated into our private-school program in California.

Many of the techniques which I had observed as being successful in the school programs in Russia, China, Japan, Taiwan, and Philippines were techniques which I would soon incorporate into our own private-school curriculum. The biggest question would be whether or not we would be able to balance our high level of creative expression in writing, art, music, and drama with the more traditional and exhaustive teaching routines which I had observed.

Then there is also the contrasting emphasis upon teaching methodology in the colleges and universities in our state of California as contrasted with Columbia, University of Northern Iowa, or perhaps universities in other countries. This fact is evidenced by the hundreds of interviews which I have given to applicants who have attended four or five years of college in California, received their credentials, and still did not know how to begin to teach or relate well to children. There seems to be a disconnect between most college coursework and the necessary teaching techniques, classroom management, time scheduling, psychology of motivating children, discipline techniques, and lesson planning that are necessary in order to become a good teacher.

Outstanding teacher-training programs stress teaching methodology coursework up front with 72 to 100 units of required educational methodology courses prior to completing a liberal arts requirement for a bachelor's degree. Currently, in California the opposite is required whereby students earn their bachelor's degree in liberal arts and then take an additional year in pursuit of a teaching credential. It is my opinion that this fifth year is too little, too late. The liberal arts program is simply an advanced level of high school, and four years later it appears to me that college students are too old to assimilate the basic teaching strategies which are necessary for teaching-style development. Usually, teaching applicants who have taken their teaching methodology coursework after the completion of the bachelor's degree are unsure of how to teach or even unsure as to whether or not teaching might be the correct career for them. One example that sticks in my mind was a very well-qualified, lovely, capable-appearing applicant who was very impressive in her first interview. I require a second part to our interview system which allows the applicant to present an impromptu fifteen-to-twenty minute age-appropriate sample lesson to a group of our students. This sample lesson can be anything of their choice such as reading a story, teaching a simple math lesson, or a get-acquainted question-and-answer period. The particular young lady whom I just mentioned stepped out in front of a kindergarten group of children who were sitting and listening intently as she introduced herself. She then turned to me at the back of the classroom and said, "I really can't think of anything to say to these children," after which she walked away and probably never went for another interview or teaching position in her life. Unfortunately for her, she had spent five years earning her education and her teaching credential but was unable or unprepared to actually relate to children.

A third step to our interview process involves the children present in the sample-lesson presentation. Quizzing the students later reveals many characteristics which the adult interviewer would probably not notice. Questioning the students as to how they felt about the prospective teacher (was she or he interesting? Would you like to have this teacher come and visit your class again for a whole day?) reveals how quickly students bond with an applicant. It also reveals the depth of communication or relating skills which this person possesses. Furthermore, group-management skills are evident from the very first minute that a prospective teacher walks in front of a group of students. Some applicants present a short speech, oblivious to the wandering interest of children. Some are frustrated at any interruption or question from a child. All these characteristics are noted, and the most successful applicant is the one who is well qualified, enjoys, and relates well to a group of children.

Based upon this three-part-interview style, we have selected wonderful teachers who with additional training and excellent curriculum guides are able to successfully educate our students to their highest potential. We believe that we definitely have found the ingredients that bring about self-motivation and successful test scores. The politically driven public system which ties professional teaching careers to tenure, short teaching schedules, lack of motivation, and accountability of their students is not about to change. I commend President Bush for his attempt to improve education by his "No Child Left Behind" campaign, but I doubt that this band-aid will raise the educational standing of the United States from 47 to possibly even 46. It's not adding more money or even new programs that are needed; it's all about upgrading our teacher-training programs, selecting teachers in advance with whom children relate, eliminating the poorly trained teachers who lack initiative and the wherewithal to motivate and teach children. We need to hire teachers who know how to utilize high expectations for each and every child in order to raise the level of education in our classrooms and in our country.

CHAPTER 32

NEW ALLEGATIONS WREAK HAVOC

E verything seemed to be returning to normal in the school business after the insurance company made such a sizeable settlement with those children in the alleged molestation cases. During the summer of 1987, I had planned to take a week off in August and spend that time on the ranch which I now owned in Fallbrook, California, after purchasing it from my mother. I drove to the preschool on Pacific Avenue early that morning to make sure that everything was in order for the week. Upon entering the office, I noticed that all four telephone lines were lit up, and several teachers who were standing in the office holding a newspaper seemed unusually startled as I entered. The first question that I remember being asked by the director was "Did you read the morning paper?"

"No," I answered. "But why are all of the phone lines on hold?" I asked. The director answered, "Well, one of the lines is your mother." Fearing that something had happened to her, I said that I wanted to talk with her first. After answering that phone line, my mother frantically asked, "Is it true?" She seemed so upset and almost irrational that I put two and two together and told her that I would read the newspaper and call her back. The headlines on the *Press-Telegram,* Long Beach, California/Thursday, August 20, 1987 read, "6-year-old girl survives torching, mother killed; McKinney preschool employee, man are booked for murder" The front-page article continued by stating that the woman, Glynnis McKinney a Long Beach preschool employee and her male companion were arrested and booked for murder, attempted murder and kidnapping. The article further stated that Glynnis McKinney's mother was the owner of McKinney School and the child who was torched apparently attended the preschool. A sheriff's department spokesman Sam Jones indicated that the school was owned by McKinney's mother, who was forced to resign a state committee post in 1985 after an employee at the McKinney School in Long Beach pleaded guilty to five counts of child molestation.

Dragging the McKinney School name into this front page article and further connecting the former molestation cases as well as the information about my being forced to resign from the state committee post in 1985 was truly unconscionable. Taking the last name of the alleged murderer and combining that name with the name of our school and then dragging up the plea bargain from our earlier inconclusive prematurely settled molestation case along with the additional forced resignation of my state appointed committee post appeared to be malicious defamation.

Immediately I placed a call to my attorney and ordered him to draw up a lawsuit against the *Press-Telegram*. Not only did the reporter who wrote the story know me personally, but I also had seen him in the courthouse during the molestation trial. He knew full well that I was Caucasian and the actual murderer was an African American woman who he stated was my daughter. The murder and torching of the child took place in Compton at a home day-care center which is definitely not a school, much less a school which was well-known and with a good reputation in Long Beach.

I was angry at the political undertones which motivated these false accusations. I knew that several Democrats were running for political office, and if they could undermine my Republican reputation which was aligned with the Republican Party they could finally damage our school the way they believed it should have been damaged and even closed down at the time of the molestation accusations. The stakes were high, but I was not willing to let the negative false reporting smear the reputation of our finest elementary school.

The legal battle was hot and heavy. My attorney fees were escalating, and there seemed to be no end in sight.

Those four or five years soon became a blur with the hysteria heightened to such frenzy that it required all my attention and many thousands of dollars. Again I sat intently listening in long-drawn-out depositions. This lawsuit also began gaining momentum.

I was invited by the owner of the *Press-Telegram*, Dan Ritter, to meet him personally in his private office, but he required that I must go alone, without my attorney. That meeting in which he tried again and again to force me to drop my lawsuit was complete bribery and a failure on his part. The *Press-Telegram* building was rather stark and cold, but upon entering his plush office, I felt intentionally intimidated but to no avail. I refused to buy into his reasoning that the *Press-Telegram* had done nothing wrong. He told me that as a reasonable citizen, I should not be causing the *Press-Telegram* to spend more than the two million dollars to defend themselves against my case. I did not back down and eventually won a $75,000 settlement in this lawsuit against the *Press-Telegram*. Of course not only was my award and settlement *never* mentioned in the newspaper, but there was never an apology to me personally or any mention in the news that the dozen or more damaging articles in the newspaper were completely false. Additionally, the *Press-Telegram* was required as part of the settlement to print several articles which would be favorable to our school, which they never did. Over $70,000 of my settlement was needed to pay my attorney fees, but more than anything, I was thankful that the ordeal was over and that the case was proven to be completely false.

CHAPTER 33

BALANCING ACTS IN LIFE

A very important skill in life is the one which allows a person to be engaged in focusing on more than one project at the same time. I found that it became critically important to be able to compartmentalize my thinking and my energies. Often I would find that a number of priorities were at the top of the list. One way which I found to be helpful was to take a full sheet of paper and list the major areas in which I had involvement. These might be as follows: family, business, finances, ranch, pets, church activities, and exercise. Then I would list everything which needed to be done that very day or as soon as possible. After sorting through my to-do list, I would prioritize the categories. Now it was time to check everything off on my list as fast as possible. There were many times that a few items on my list of fifty or sixty items had to be extended to a second or even a third day; however, the faster I checked off each item, the better I would feel about getting my life in order.

Without a checklist, it would have been impossible to properly organize and efficiently complete all of the tasks for which I had taken responsibility in a given day or week. I remember that there were times when I had listed over a hundred tasks which must all be completed yesterday so to speak. Using this system was the only way that I found to conquer such a multitude of tasks. Later on, I found that the art of delegation is a good discipline to master. In fact, at one time it became a joke that I could delegate more tasks than anyone else in this business could. One thing I learned about delegating is that you never want to delegate anything that you do not personally know how to do or are willing to accomplish by yourself. When computers first came out, we were one of the first schools to provide a computer lab in our school. We started out with fourteen Texas Instrument computers and designated one of our teachers who had already been taking computer courses in college to become the computer-lab teacher. I thought to myself, *This is one thing that I will hire someone else to do*. I felt that I did not want to take the time to bother learning a new skill which sounded quite complex to me. Well, that didn't last long. Finally, I took one of the computers and the instruction manual home for a weekend and learned how to use it fairly well in that one weekend. Later on, I remembered again that I must never require an employee to do or teach anything that I could not do or would not be willing to do; otherwise, I could not be a good supervisor, much less be able to understand any of the problems that each employee encountered. This was also true in the early years when we were short on funds and I needed to request that our teachers vacuum their classrooms and clean the kitchen and the restrooms for their respective areas. There were a few who balked; however, when they observed that I was doing their assigned job, simply because we could not afford custodial assistance, they softened. It became effective for them to see that their boss was doing what they considered a job beneath their dignity to perform. We were thankful to those who pitched in and rose to the occasion during those hard times. Today we have teaching assistants, regional occupational program assistants, and custodial services in each of our school facilities. We also no longer cook our meals and wash dishes; we contract for food services to cater for our students. We have come a long way since those early days, and our employees appreciate the supportive services which we are now able to provide.

CHAPTER 34

HOUR OF POWER

There were many times when the weight of the world seemed to be on my shoulders. Years of being put down and being rejected because of my divorce left me feeling like the story of the woman in the Bible whose accusers stoned her to death. Jesus said to the accusers, "Let he who is without sin, cast the first stone," and they silently walked away in shame. Soon I stopped attending church because of the negativism.

One Sunday morning as I relaxed in my backyard, I began to yearn for Christian fellowship. I turned on a little five-inch television I had in the patio and scanned the stations until I came to a station where a minister was preaching a Christian message with a positive and accepting tone. I would learn later that this was Dr. Robert H. Schuller. He was inspiring and positive as he spoke words of encouragement. I wrote down the phone number and called to find out the location of their church. It turned out to be a drive-in church, and I could go there and listen in my car and not have to be exposed to rejection or scrutiny as to why I was a single mom with children, the divorced wife of a minister, etc. It was of interest to me that Dr. Schuller was also from Iowa. He came to California in the same year when we made our first long trip to California. Interestingly enough, he also came to California with a goal to preach and become a pastor much the same as we had done. It certainly was our hope and prayer to be in Christian ministry in California. He began preaching in an abandoned drive-in theater, and that church ministry grew year after year. Later they built a new church building which they named the Crystal Cathedral.

While attending the Crystal Cathedral, I met happy, radiant, and even beautiful people who accepted me as a person. I was overwhelmed by their love and caring acceptance. I was overflowing with tears by just feeling their love and acceptance. I attended a divorce-recovery meeting; and between the positive messages from the sermons, their Christian literature, and my new praying friends, my tears began to heal. I remembered discussing the negative approach which was spoken in the church at the time my husband's ministerial position was terminated. I argued that certainly there should be a more positive approach to the message of salvation. It seemed important to me that children should be taught the positive aspects of Christianity, and then I believed that children would more readily accept the plan of salvation rather than coming to Christianity because of fear or rejection. Telling children and people in general that they are sinful and their hearts are black with sin always seemed too negative and judgmental. That approach, in my opinion, seemed to cause people to shrink away and reject the message of the Bible which is that God sent His Son for every person to follow Him, believe in Him, and turn from their sinful nature. He would then give them the gift of Salvation. Salvation means that a new spiritual nature or a new life would overwrite or transform the soul. It would be much the same as gaining a fresh new outlook or, as is often referred to, as having a new birth experience. That experience is what Christians refer to as being "born again." The former natural, human, or sinful nature and personality tending toward negative thinking and evil intentions would be cleared away and as if a new software program would be instantly installed which would have spiritual inclinations, admiration and heartfelt connections or bonding with God; His Son, Jesus Christ; and the Holy Spirit.

Dr. Schuller often received criticism whereby people believed that he was only preaching positive thinking rather than preaching the plan of salvation. The *Hour of Power*, he said, was similar to a commercial on television which was reaching out to hurting people and providing a message. This message would allow them to hear the true story of the Bible and accept God's positive plan for their life. Salvation healing and growth in knowledge would follow. Love, peace, acceptance, fulfillment, joy, and happiness are trademarks of a real Christian.

It is truly thrilling that the *Hour of Power* is now reaching into nearly every country in the world with the message of God. I believe that this message will someday change the hearts of millions of people. Christian nations would be more loving, caring, and peaceful. This possibility gives a lot of hope for the future, and I am happy to encourage people to listen to the *Hour of Power*. This one program changed my life, bringing a new freedom, acceptance, and happiness into my life. It was due to this change in my emotional outlook that allowed me to overcome unbelievable obstacles and oppression. I can never thank Dr. Schuller enough for driving with his wife from Iowa to California in 1955 to begin a church in a little old drive-in theater. His life is truly a testimonial as to how God can lead and bless a person who is obedient. His testimony enabled me as well as probably hundreds and thousands of people throughout the world to hear the true Christian message that God sent His Son Jesus to provide salvation to all who would believe in Him thus giving each believer a Heavenly relationship with God. All things are possible to those who believe. Thank you, Dr. Schuller, for obeying God's calling despite the many obstacles which you met.

Additionally, I can't help think of the contrast in the life of Dr. Schuller as contrasted with my minister husband. Both men were from Iowa and had graduated from colleges with bachelor degrees and then seminary with divinity degrees. Both drove to California in 1955 or 1956 with the intention of serving as a minister of God. Both had the expectation of being successful as ministers. What were the predicting factors in their lives which caused such a divergence from that point on? Certainly, each claimed God as their Heavenly Father, and both believed the Bible. Both had a born-again experience. Both had studied Greek and Hebrew and the history of the Christian church. Both had supportive, talented Christian wives. Both had loving children. Always I will ponder the question as to why one had a thriving ministry and the other was forced into abandoning the ministry. God does work in mysterious ways, and we as humans can never understand the rationale or the reasons for such a dramatic difference between two graduating seminary students regarding their future ministries. It reminds me of the weaver who when working on the threads from underneath the cloth can only appreciate the scene when looking at the topside of the beautiful tapestry.

I am thrilled that the *Hour of Power* as well as other Christian ministries are being aired throughout the world and that there are testimonies of conversions in every country. I believe that God is using His message and this form of media as well as the hourofpower.org on the Internet to reach millions of people who are hurting and searching for God. It pleases me to be a small part of this endeavor by making contributions, however large or small. I believe that God is carrying out his purpose through Christian ministries like this one.

Left to right: Bonnie (friend of David) Jon Christianson, son of Nancy, David Henry (Phyllis's youngest son, Cathy Jones (Phyllis's daughter), Dorothy Kellogg (Phyllis's mother) Phyllis and Ken Duke (bride and groom), Van Dera (wife of Curtis Henry (Phyllis's oldest son, Connie Christianson (daughter of Nancy), Todd, husband of Connie, Nancy (sister of Phyllis, Bob Pedersen, husband of Nancy.

Front row of Phyllis's grandchildren: Spencer, Lauren and Erin Henry and Monica and Wyatt Jones.

CHAPTER 35

RECOGNIZING MATURE LOVE

Young people tend to pick a partner similar to themselves or to their own parents. Very often in studying strangers in a large crowd, I can notice obvious physical characteristics and similarities in the outward appearance and even in the personalities of couples. There will most often be striking facial similarities. I remember that my own mother thought that the only person for me to marry would be a man who was tall with dark brown eyes and hair just like my father. Anyone not meeting her initial criteria was instantly rejected by her in a most abrupt and obvious manner. Secondly, this prospective suitor would need to be a Christian leader of notable reputation and needed to be musically inclined. I think parental influences weigh more heavily in whom a person chooses to date than that person would ever admit or realize.

"Puppy love" was never really explained or understood by teenagers when I was growing up. Instead there was a Cinderella myth about the man who might enter one's life, on a white horse, if you will. Neither of these attractions will ever be helpful in selecting a right person to date or in the development of a right relationship. Now mind you, I was well educated, talented, considered somewhat good looking with a fun-loving personality. What I needed help with was fending off the boys and/or later the young men who were persistent, pushy, and wanting only their own personal gratification. I did fairly well in eliminating pushy suitors and remained a virgin until my marriage; however, this negative pressure placed each and every relationship in an awkward tug-of-war. Never was there a man who understood my feelings or who would say, "I understand and agree how important abstinence is prior to building a solid relationship, teamwork skills, financial planning, and working toward building a life and a future family together." If this could ever have happened, I would have had an opportunity to stand back and truly evaluate the true depth of our feelings for each other as well as to study how compatible we were or what kind of a team we could make if we joined and worked toward a future life together. Since none of that ever happened in my dating relationships. I was left with wondering how much pressure I could tolerate and finally succumb as it seemed that I was always needed in order for the other person to feel satisfied and thus survive in life. I finally gave in and decided that I would make the best of a relationship because the person with needs would never go away. I decided that I would commit myself to this person in a similar manner as I would have committed myself to becoming a dedicated missionary for that cause. I began to rationalize that, after all, this person was tall, with dark brown eyes and hair. Isn't that what my mother told me was important? Wasn't this person interested in preparing for Christian ministry? Couldn't I just finally give in and accept him in marriage? After all, hadn't he desperately pursued me at every single turn? I was beginning to feel like used merchandise. Would the wonderful man I had hoped for in my life even ever accept me now . . . as a person who had been involved in an unhealthy relationship against my best judgment and my will? I had already broken off this relationship twice, but this one had maneuvered his way back into my life with more pressure and control than ever before. Hadn't he already moved into the home of my parents in an effort to get me to marry him? Hadn't he threatened me with an ultimatum to marry him within two months or else? Why did I become defensive when other people questioned my judgment in marrying him? Why couldn't I foresee the lifetime of pain and torture that I might suffer simply because I was being pressured into an incompatible relationship? Hadn't I already looked into his family background? Why couldn't I use the red flags that I began to recognize in order to call for help so that I might escape from this relationship and the imminent upcoming danger? How could my sympathy for him cause me to sacrifice my own ideals in life in what turned out to be an unhealthy and out-of-balance relationship and marriage?

Clearly, marriage must have components of friendship, mutual respect, admiration, a teamwork approach to living life together, true love, and a genuine commitment to each other. Without those ingredients, any marriage will ultimately fail. Currently, marriages are failing at the rate of 50 percent or one out of every two in today's cultural times. Students are taught everything else in school and college except the skills of how to build a foundation for a successful marriage.

After many years of being single and vowing to never marry again, I knew I had finally met someone with whom I could trust and build that solid relationship which could develop into marriage. When we both were sixty, we joined our lives in holy matrimony. Our marriage of sixteen years has taught me the meaning of real love, shared teamwork, and goals. He reminds me daily that he loves me for better or worse and no matter what happens, and that unconditional love is like a solid rock foundation for our wonderful marriage. To have him share in my goals in life as well as for me to assist him in reaching his goals has become a teamwork approach which I never experienced before. A time or two when my Irish temper begins to flare up due to something he did or said, I found that he would turn to me and say "I love you." It's hardly possible to feel angry when someone is gently saying they love you. This, I believe, is a true mark of unconditional love. He allows me be myself and respects me for my differences. This soothing support system allows us to do things in life which we never would have thought possible. Are we perfect? No, but we know that we are part of a team and we respect and care for each other. Being part of a team with mutual goals, love, and respect for each other is truly what marriage is all about.

It has been said that if one person has to be propped up by the other, that person can never become a team partner in marriage. A person can look the part, be willing to accept all the love and support that can possibly be given to him or her; but if that person cannot stand alone, he could never be part of a team. Eventually such a frail union or marriage will fall apart. Evidently, there are millions of fragile marriages out there that sooner or later will fall apart. If two people are rowing a boat side by side and the one on the left continues to row with long, strong strides and the one on the right is weak or does not row, the boat will go in circles and eventually the strong rower will become exhausted and stop rowing. It's also like building a house on sand, and when the rains come, it will fall down. It won't make any difference how attractive two people look together. It won't make any difference if one person gives 110 percent to the marriage and the other only gives 10 percent . . . It will fail sooner or later. After a marriage falls apart, the troubles have only just begun especially when there are children involved. The children can never understand nor easily forgive their parents for getting into a faulty marriage that truly had no foundation. They can never understand why they have to be torn between two parents. Neither can they understand or even want to believe that one parent might not have been strong enough or mature enough to build a successful marriage and a solid family for them as children. The "fallout" continues for the lifetime of each child, grandchild, and probably even future great-grandchildren. It will span generations. The pain only diminishes and goes into remission for small periods during a lifetime. It recurs at the time of the illness of one or the other of the children, family reunions, marriages, and even at the time of the death of one or the other spouse or children. A broken marriage can never be repaired. It is for this reason that I believe there should be a better way to educate teenagers while they are young and while they are contemplating their future. There must be better road signs for the next generation. Young people must be taught how to recognize a compatible, suitable mate in order to guarantee a successful marriage. Otherwise, possibly there should be a very costly insurance plan which would guarantee a successful marriage. I would even go so far as to say that a license should be required which would make a poor or mismatched marriage financially prohibitive. We respect the need for a good education. Degrees, certificates, and also exams are required in order to practice in professions such as doctors, lawyers, and teachers. These high requirements are required to obtain employment in many occupations. It is of grave concern that there are no requirements to give birth to a child and only a marriage license for a mere few dollars is required in order to get married. Wouldn't it seem that the highest calling in life should be to marry, have a family, and nurture that family and those children until they are able to become independent and continue that practice for generation after generation? Should the requirements be a minimum of a two-year degree in Marriage Course 101 and then an additional degree in Child Birth and Family Management 101 prior to giving birth to any baby? If an automobile company produces cars by trial and error with no scientific basis, would we be purchasing those cars? I believe that we place a greater emphasis on registering and training dogs and horses than we place on quality parenting and training of our children.

CHAPTER 36

PHYSICAL FITNESS FOR HEALTH AND LONGEVITY

It has been shown in research that the more physically active a young child is prior to age eight, the healthier he or she will be when older. This is very important when it comes to assessing the physical needs of young children. Parents need to evaluate the damage caused by the amount of time that their children spend watching television or being sedentary. It might be possible to project the health of that child by studying his or her daily activity level. Based upon this theory, I believe that my active childhood helped predetermine the level of good health which I have been able to enjoy in my fifties, sixties, and now seventies.

The childhood activities which kept me active and moving were ice skating; roller skating; skiing; climbing trees; running through the woods on animal-finding expeditions; and caring for chickens, ducks, and other animals on our farm. It is truly amazing how active a child can be when there is a purpose.

Suggested activities for the city-dwelling children might include walking a dog two to three miles twice a day; riding a bicycle for several hours; and being involved in swimming, soccer, or softball clubs. Participating in cleaning activities inside or outside the house could also be an exercising activity. Perhaps the most important aspect about evaluating the activity level of any specific child would be to ascertain the amount of time he or she is sitting or being uninvolved in physical activities each day.

Needless to say, no level of activity would be a substitute for a nutritious diet. It would not be possible for a child who lives on pizza, pasta, cookies, and ice cream to be able to sustain a healthful exercise regime. The bursts of energy received from a carbohydrate diet are spent by the body almost as quickly as the time it takes to eat those foods. Those are empty carbohydrates which will ultimately cause the death of many cells in the body. The child trying to live on white bread, white sugar, and a high-carbohydrate diet will sooner or later look pale, lack sparkling eyes, fall asleep easily during the day, require lots of sleep, have frequent headaches, and become listless. It takes as many as seven or eight servings of fruit; vegetables; and protein in nuts, beans, and meat every day in order to build strong muscles with lasting endurance.

CHAPTER 37

REVERSE CAREGIVER ROLES

N ever in one's lifetime can a person become emotionally prepared for a reversal in the care giving roles of life. When a new mother learns to care for her baby, she becomes aware of the great responsibilities which she must now assume. There is so much to learn, and the consequences are so great. Signals such as crying, gas pains, and fever are important; and each one means something. The baby cannot talk; and the mother must learn when to feed her baby, burp the baby to relieve gas pains, change the diaper, and provide proper warmth and clothing. All these new signals and tasks are taken in stride. Suddenly there is also a keen interest in the stories and experiences of other new mothers and a new interest in reading everything about caring for babies that has been ever written on the subject.

My children were still quite young when Dr. Spock's books about caring for babies and young children were published. His books were considered as valuable to young mothers as the Bible was considered for believers or churchgoers. Whether Dr. Spock was right or wrong, almost everyone who read his book followed his advice to the letter. This, of course, backfired on many families because Dr. Spock's position on discipline was basically to let the child do whatever feels good and not to correct or punish the child. The idea was to avoid inhibiting the developing personality of the young child.

Sometimes in life, that caregiver role becomes reversed. It happened in my life after my father passed away; I soon realized that he had been the business head in our family. Even though I had seen my mother purchase things and write checks, I never knew that she did not balance the checkbook. What a shock! I thought I could teach her very quickly since I knew that she had always been very astute in mathematics, but I didn't realize how difficult it would be. She never seemed to grasp the complete idea that the amount of money deposited in the bank had to balance with the total of the amount of the checks written and, as that, related to whether or not some of the checks had been cashed or not. This was the beginning of my role of trying to oversee the management of her affairs. That was only the very beginning of a twenty-eight-year responsibility of becoming her caregiver.

My first efforts to assist with overseeing the financial management for my mother were very minimal compared to the more accelerated levels of care which became necessary during her last two to five years of her life. She had been managing her home beautifully; entertaining her many friends, church-related groups; and overseeing maintenance and repairs, gardening, and other neighborly duties. Her first health-related problem came at age eight-seven when she fell and broke her kneecap. This accident on the sidewalk in front of her home required surgery, several days of bed rest, and then the use of a walker. She was still living alone in her home and generally refused to have anyone live with her or even to use her walker when she was required to do so. It became obvious to me that she was becoming unable to care for herself and manage her home and gardens. I had begun noticing that she would go to lunch at Arnold's Restaurant and then take home enough food to warm up for several additional meals. Then when I stopped in to visit her, I would check the refrigerator and began seeing signs of mold and food spoilage. She seemed to have lost her ability to determine when food was fresh or even to remember to clean her refrigerator.

The next step was to encourage my mother to move into an assisted living complex where meals and cleaning of her apartment would be done for her regularly. This was a big step and one which she was unwilling to take. She did not want to accept an invitation to move into my home even though I had prepared a room just for her. I had gone to great lengths to adorn her walls with her memorabilia in preparation for the possibility that she might need care someday. It turned out that the Christian and

Missionary Alliance church which our family attended when I was a child growing up in Mason City, Iowa, had decided to build a retirement center for their returning missionaries. This beautiful facility was located in Santa Ana, California. I visited the facility and found that there were several residents in that facility whom my mother knew from among her church friends. She had begun to say that if she ever had to move into a care facility, the Town and Country Manor which was the one built by the Christian and Missionary Alliance Association would be the only one she would consider. I had checked out several others, and I did agree that the Town and Country Manor seemed to be ideal. Finally I made an appointment and took my mother for an interview and a tour of the manor. She also was impressed. She toured the only unfurnished one-room suite that was available. It was on the second floor, a fairly large room, maybe 14' by 22", with private bathroom, a small kitchenette, two large closets, and a west-facing sliding-glass door which opened into a small deck. She really liked that particular room.

There was a long screening procedure by which the board of directors of the manor would determine whom they would allow into the manor. After all, we were told this project was built for retiring missionaries; and even though they were extending invitations to outsiders, they were being very particular in who they would accept. I filled out the entrance questionnaire for Mother, and then we waited for what was expected to be a three-week screening process. Very soon, perhaps the very next day, I received a phone call in which the woman who had interviewed my mother told me that several of the people at the manor, and even some on the board of directors, knew my mother and that she could enter the manor immediately if she would accept the only room which was available at that time. That was the same room which she had seen, and it was the one which was available. Perhaps this was the pressure that my mother needed because she very much did like that room with its view of westerly sunsets, and if she didn't take it, she might not get a room later on that she liked that much. The other determining factor was the rule that if she didn't enter the manor prior to needing a more intensive level of care, she would not be allowed to enter later at level 2 or when she might need intensive care. This was very important because there was always the possibility of a stroke or a heart attack since my mother had extremely high blood pressure, had hypoglycemia, and could have another serious fall or even a prolonged illness similar to what my father endured for eighteen months with congestive heart failure prior to his death.

Moving my mother from a two-bedroom home with a garage full of accumulated clutter was horrendous. It seemed as if she went into a trance regarding the move. She would, literally, stand in the middle of the living room while I made every decision regarding what items to pack, what furniture to move, and what items should be given to her children or grandchildren, even goodwill. Maybe she was in greater need of help and assistance than anyone realized. We moved her white sofa bed so she could invite overnight guests, her oak bedroom set, her walnut china closet, and the cedar chest which my father had built for her soon after they were married. I selected the clothing I felt she would need much as if she were going to be taking a long vacation. I packed the ruby glassware and the best of her dishes, silverware, and pots and pans. I knew that she probably would never be cooking again, but cooking had been one of her greatest loves in life and we didn't want her to feel deprived. This turned out to be only the first of five moves that she would make in the following nine months. Each time we narrowed her personal things down to less furniture, no cookware or dishes, etc. Each move was brought about by the need for more intensive care following a broken shoulder, then a broken hip, and even an illness which placed her into a coma for a short time. She seemed to lose more and more of her ability to care for herself and even to know what to do in her daily routine.

During those last two years of this time when mother was in the Town and Country Manor or other care facilities, my husband, Ken, who was a real estate agent, and I worked to paint and repair her home and prepare it for sale. We even arranged a short-term rental for two visiting teachers whom I had hired from Canada. That meant furnishing the house for them and cleaning it again after their departure. Finally, the house sold, but at a very low price due to the low real estate values in the depressed Long Beach area at that time. If we could have held that house another three years, we could have received double the price; and as of this date, the price would be tripled. But no one knew the future of real estate, and the house was becoming a real burden to care for and keep rented.

My mother had many heart wrenching experiences in three different convalescent care facilities and two hospitals as well as problems with her insurance coverage. She cried daily and begged me to take her out of the last facility, Rowland Heights Convalescent Home in order to move her into my home and live with us. This was a very difficult decision for me. She was ninety years of age, and her mind had begun showing evidence of dementia. She was 85 percent paralyzed from a stroke which she suffered on July 5, the morning after she watched fireworks from her window at the Palm Crest Rest Home in Long Beach. She was only staying there for one week while we made a trip with two other couples to Colorado. She had enjoyed short visits at the Palm Crest other times, allowing us to take short trips. She always enjoyed her short stays there. She had already been living in my home for a year, a period in which I hired different relatives to help as caregivers. They lived in a section of our house which we had organized as a private apartment especially for mother and her caretakers. This worked quite well for that year, but Mother's mind was failing and it was somewhat difficult for her caregivers to be patient with her requests and demands as well as her problems with dementia.

During that next to the last year of Mother's life, I tried to allow her independence while still managing her affairs. Approximately a year prior to that, she had reluctantly handed her checkbook to me and said, "You might as well handle it all." But during that year when she lived with us and while she was still quite mobile, we took her on many outings; trips; dinner dates with my youngest sister, Nancy; and many of mother's best friends. We arranged for breakfast at a small restaurant overlooking Newport Beach, a luncheon or dinner at Knott's Berry Farm, and many other special occasions. Mother always lived in the moment and truly loved being with family and friends. She was also an avid Scrabble player. She always seemed to be able to win every game until the week of her passing away except maybe one at the Town and Country Manor, where evidently her reputation as a champion was challenged by one elderly gentleman. She thought, however, that maybe he didn't play fairly; and I'm not sure if she ever played Scrabble with that person again.

Mother enjoyed our flowers, fruit trees, and our garden. She always wanted to walk around behind our garage, where Ken had built a raised vegetable garden with railroad ties surrounding it. The soil on our property is totally red clay or sandstone, so in order to have healthy fruit trees or a garden, we had black soil delivered. Mother could stay by the garden for hours admiring each plant if we would let her. She walked with a walker around our house on the sidewalk many times a day, but it always took some encouragement to keep her walking enough for an adequate amount of daily exercise. The caretakers would find reasons to keep her walking, and she did quite well until the stroke hit her on July 5.

I had received a call while we were on vacation from the Palm Crest Rest Home early on the morning of July 5. I directed the nurse who found her on the floor at about seven that morning to call an ambulance and take her to a hospital in West Covina which was covered by her insurance plan. We packed immediately and our guests were forced to leave also and we drove directly back to Long Beach. Finding Mother in a condition in which she could not talk or swallow, which lasted for about seven or almost eight days, was difficult. The doctor spoke to me about arranging to place her in a hospice facility in the event that she was unable to eat or swallow on the eighth day. I visited the hospice in order to make arrangements. While I was there, I learned that patients who are sent there are not expected to live for more than a few hours or days and that the family members can sit or sleep there in the room giving extra comfort. There would be no further treatment for her condition, only medication to ease her pain. On the eighth day, however, Mother miraculously began eating and swallowing. She was now paralyzed on her left side including the left muscles in her neck, back, left arm, and left leg. Since she improved so much by the ninth day, the doctors advised me to find a convalescent home where she could be cared for in this condition. After much research, my son Curtis and his wife, Van, found the Rowland Heights Convalescent Home, which would accept her.

A new quandary began. The insurance company would not cover expenses in the convalescent home except for the time in which Mother was kept on intravenous feeding. This became a disastrous time because if Mother was taken off intravenous feeding, she was still unable to lift her head to drink, reach for a glass, or feed herself. The nurses would invariably place her food or drink on a rolling table too far away from her. Even with a good arm she could not have reached the table. I finally hired a private nurse assistant to stay with her for eight to ten hours each day. Every day after work when I visited her, I would find her crying and begging to go home with me. It was difficult for me to drive an extra hour each way every day and enter the convalescent home with its odors, see all kinds of people in there (many in much worse condition than my mother), and additionally try to help and visit with her roommate and all of her many problems. It simply wasn't working for me. Mother was crying and begging to go home with me every time I saw her. Finally, I reluctantly agreed to take her home with me. Just moving her was a monumental task. It took at least two or three strong people, a hoist, a long extended reclining wheelchair, and the right timing between meals and bathroom necessities in order to move her. Additionally, she often became dizzy and would vomit when moved; but bravely, I had the nurses prepare her for the trip in my car and I took on the full responsibility for caring for my mother, now an invalid, 85 percent paralyzed, and with early dementia.

The first week with my mother in that condition was horrendous. We had tied two single beds together so that I could rest next to her. She needed to be turned over frequently and have a change of clothing and had constant need for food, juice, and water. Turning over a person weighing 165 pounds and who could not use their own muscles was extremely difficult. It was simply more than I could do physically. I began aching everywhere and became desperate for a solution. I slept on the edge of her bed and was at her beck and call for about a week and a half. It seemed like an eternity to me. Finally, I found a list of caregiver services. This list had been given to me by the nurses when she was hospitalized. I began calling each of the services to find out if I could hire a nurse or a caregiver. Of course, there had been no insurance coverage since the last time she needed intravenous feeding, and Mother's meager funds from the sale of her home were rapidly diminishing. Finally, a miracle happened. After calling many different kinds of services, I found a home health-care service called Continuing Care, where the lady asked me all kinds of questions about my mother, her personality, her condition, etc. It was not more than an hour later when the lady called me back and asked if I would accept an African American lady. I had not thought about inviting an African American to live in my home before, but I did not have a problem with it. The lady's name was Elaine, and she was sure she would like the job. It would cost approximately $2,000 per month, and she would live in the adjoining bedroom next to my mother. She would cook the meals, bathe and care for Mother as well as read to her and watch television with her. Elaine would work for three weeks on and then have one week off while a substitute within their company would relieve her. This was a big miracle!

There were groceries to shop for Mother and Elaine and medical supplies to keep in stock. Most of all, my presence was still needed almost at all times. During the full year of this kind of arrangement, I felt I could not do enough, fast enough, to meet the demands on me. Mother's mind improved immensely whereby she wondered why I worked so much, why I was often ten minutes late coming to see her, why I couldn't take her for a ride, why I couldn't have guests in to visit her more often. She asked why I couldn't play the piano or organ and sing for her more often, etc. When I did play the piano for her, she would request the old-time favorite hymns that we had sung when I played the piano when I was only six to eight years old. Somehow, the emotions which this brought out would be more than I could handle. Tears would be streaming down my face as I would reflect on her life and the suffering which she was enduring. She was always happy and smiling even in this condition. I could hardly bear the thought. Praying with her was also difficult for me. It seemed almost unfathomable that any human being should have to suffer the way she was in a body that was barely functioning but in which her mind became sharper every day she lived with us.

Mother loved to have Ken read books to her. He graciously accepted the challenge, and night after night he read whole chapters of several different books to her. The book she enjoyed the most was the autobiography by Dr. Schuller. She was thrilled to hear about his life growing up on a farm in Iowa and how God had blessed him and guided him throughout his ministry. Day after day she received encouragement and spiritual strength from the inspirational stories which Dr. Schuller wrote about in his book. Sometimes she would appear to fall asleep, but when Ken would stop reading, she would ask him to keep reading because she said that she was only resting her eyes. I also had several videos of the *Hour of Power*, which she watched over and over again. These replays of the *Hour of Power* literally gave strength and encouragement to her throughout the full year in which she was paralyzed.

Mother had been accustomed to driving her own car and traveling throughout the world up until she was eighty-nine years old. In fact, it was when she was ninety that she failed to receive a renewed driver's license. She always believed that the motor vehicle department had a ruling that they would not issue a license to anyone who is ninety or older. I guess thinking that way salvaged her self-image because I later found a copy of her driver exam and noted that she really did not pass the test. She lost a lot of her initiative to travel when she was unable to drive herself and when I sold her car to some friends of hers. Somehow she thought that since the buyers of her car were friends of hers, they would always invite her to ride with them when they went somewhere. When that didn't happen, she really took it personally and she felt much rejection.

Being a caregiver was taking on new meaning for me during this time with my mother. She is the one who said it so candidly. She said, "Well, I guess I am the biggest baby you ever had to care for!" I couldn't have said it better. Taking care of an adult who had nearly the same needs as that of a newborn infant but with greater emotional needs and who had accumulated ninety-one-plus years of ongoing baggage and seventy years of a relationship between a daughter and a mother turned out to be the greatest test of survival that I had yet encountered in my life. There had been times over the years when she had challenged my integrity; my authority over her affairs; her skepticism about my relationships; her refusal to assist or support me when I had overwhelming needs as a young mother who was too poor to buy food while they had more than plenty; and then the times when she believed that I shorted her in her payments when in actuality I always had done everything in my power to help her manage, keep, and invest her money wisely. In fact, I knew that if I had not managed her money and her affairs for all those twenty-eight years, she would not have had a dime left for her own care, much less a small estate to divide with her three daughters and her five grandchildren. She turned out to be very sweet, appreciative and loving even though she had become handicapped. She had to be totally dependent on me for her very survival every minute of every day for the last nearly two years of her life. That love and sweetness certainly melted away the frustrations and misunderstandings which had come up between us during the prior years.

CHAPTER 38

GOLDEN YEARS OF FLASHBACKS

Living long enough to be able to observe family members and friends in four generations come and go is almost like reading a history book. My maternal grandfather, whom I loved very much, died suddenly from a heart attack when I was just three years old. Now when children are born, it feels as if you can actually visualize history in the making. You seem to have a little more wisdom about the world, relationships, and the need for humans to be more spiritual and live a life that is rewarding and fruitful. Life is very short, and the poem by an unknown author which my camp counselor taught me when I was a teenager still comes to mind: "Only one life, t'will soon be past, only what's done for Christ, will last!" What a synopsis of life. Maybe if more people memorized that poem early in their lives, they would take life and its brevity more seriously.

Four months after my mother passed away, my youngest sister, Nancy, also slipped from us. Now Nancy was the cutest one of the three of us sisters. Everyone adored Nancy. It made me, as the oldest sister; feel as if the affections heaped on her were silly. People loved to see her laugh and giggle. She was a Shirley Temple lookalike. Nancy remained bubbly and optimistic until her very last conscious minute of life. She always believed that somehow her doctor could pull her through all her continuing health problems. She had called me at about a quarter to five early one morning in mid-December and asked if I would drive and pick her up and take her in to the emergency room. She said she didn't want to have her husband,

Bob, take her because he had just left the prior evening to go to their ranch home in Palo Verde and maybe I would be able to help her. Of course, I realized the seriousness of this request in as much as Nancy had been suffering with an undiagnosed lung disease for nearly eight years. The cells in her lungs were becoming scarred and atrophied so that even though she was on oxygen twenty-four hours a day, she still could not receive enough oxygen to supply her blood. She, however, kept an optimistic outlook. She smiled, laughed, and always wanted to get out and about. She dearly loved her grandchildren and desired to live much longer than her sixty-five years. She loved and appreciated her husband, Bob. He was devoted and dedicated to her as he assisted in charting and monitoring her medicinal needs over her last several years. About two weeks prior to her passing, we celebrated Bob's birthday together at the Chart House overlooking Dana Harbor. It was a lovely evening and a wonderful meal. I took several digital pictures of the two of them. When I showed her the first picture, she didn't like her ponytail and she wanted to brush her long hair forward and have the picture taken again. The first picture had shown her face heavy with pain, suffering, and medication; but the second picture showed her radiant smile and her beautiful hair cascading over her shoulder. I think she was well aware of the shortness of her time to live, and she really wanted to leave a lasting impression of her loving, caring personality.

The morning that we got up quickly after that phone call and drove slightly over the speed limit, we arrived to find her casual and relaxed in her living room easy chair. She asked if I would put on her shoes; and then we walked together, carrying her oxygen tank down three flights of stairs, and entered the car where Ken was waiting with the engine running, ready to make a speedy dash to St. Anthony's Hospital in Orange County. After Nancy was settled in the car, she said that she wanted us to take her out to breakfast at Coco's Restaurant. I thought maybe we shouldn't stop for breakfast, much less drive out of our way to Coco's; but she insisted and so we reluctantly took her there. She ordered a large omelet and a cup of coffee and then slowly savored every single bite. Little did I know that this would be her last meal, and did she consciously want to enjoy it as long as she could? It was as if she was trying to forestall the inevitable ending of her life. How dramatic could it be? Again I was feeling overwhelming helplessness while watching a family member deal with the reality of the shortness of life.

Nancy's next few days were to become the most dramatic I had ever witnessed. Her doctor made the decision to use a forced reverse-breathing machine, which would require sedation so that her body would not fight the reverse-breathing effect, but he said he would try this procedure as it might allow her to gain the ability to breathe more normally again. Yes, the family agreed that this procedure could be tried in an effort to allow her more days, weeks, or even months to live. What the doctor did not say was that the sedation would place her in a semi coma in which she could never talk or respond to anything or anyone even though she would be totally aware of everything being said to her and everyone being there to comfort her. Wow, can you even imagine talking to someone who was bubbly, optimistic, and totally happy just a few minutes ago and who now will never be able to respond again? Additionally, the doctor never told us that once a patient goes on this reverse-breathing machine, they can never be taken off it. The intensity heightened as her husband, her two grown children and her four grown stepchildren, and I stood vigil for three days. We played her favorite music for her, talked to her, and I tearfully prayed over her. I even held the telephone near her ear as our sister, Peg, talked to her and prayed with her. We could tell by her brain wave responses that she, in fact, was well aware of everything that was going on. Her brain waves would become very active when she would try to respond. At one time, she shed a tear and gave the slightest hint of a smile, but we had to read the brain wave chart to know that she was indeed trying to make a response.

It had been only ten days ago since she spent a whole day with Connie, her daughter, grandchildren Christopher and Kimberly, and her close friend Mabel. She loved going to Knott's Berry Farm, and that day she rode her new blue scooter with the children taking turns on her lap, touring her most favorite place in the whole world. She had brought the pictures taken of her on her scooter with the grandchildren that day at Knott's Berry Farm, with copies for each of us, to the hospital for us to have when we would come to visit her. Unfortunately, those pictures were left in the hospital room and discarded by the staff, and no one ever saw them again.

We were granted a private viewing of the X-rays that were taken the day that we admitted Nancy to the emergency room. Her doctor pointed out that he could see less than only about one-half cubic inch of lung space which had not yet atrophied due to severe scarring. I registered shock as to how or why Nancy could live without the possibility of ever receiving a lung transplant. Yes, she could be kept alive on this reverse-breathing machine which pumped oxygen into her blood forever, but she would never have the opportunity to be conscious again, breathe on her own, talk, and laugh even one more time. Why? Her doctor must have been extending her life artificially until, as he told me, her family could adjust to her imminent passing. It was, however, becoming more than any family member could bear. Tears were flowing from each family member as they tried to comfort one another and also Nancy at the same time, realizing that she was trying to respond to them but was being kept in this semiconscious state at the doctor's behest. It was too traumatic to describe, but gradually, medication was administered to relieve the pain which Nancy would suffer when the reverse-breathing machine was to be withdrawn and silently Nancy slipped into eternity. She could no longer take a breath on her own.

Her funeral was magnificent. She looked beautiful in her knitted peacock sweater as she held three peacock feathers in her hand that gracefully draped over her shoulder. Even though the casket was never opened during the funeral, I was pleased that the funeral director opened the casket and allowed my husband and me to view her privately prior to the funeral. The large chapel was packed and very emotional as one admirer and friend after another slowly walked forward to share with the audience what Nancy had meant to them in their lives. They referred to her as the bridge that helped them cope in life and that brought happiness, relevance, and meaning to their families. They spoke about how she had always given them a token or a gift by which they will always remember and miss her. It may have been the most impressive funeral I ever attended and that because Nancy had in her suffering always thought of others and tried to make everyone else happy. Spiritually, I believe that Nancy prayed and renewed her childhood faith while in her semiconscious state. She had spent all her adult years as an independent thinker with a rebellious attitude toward her mother's admonitions for her to attend church. It had only been four months since she attended our mother's funeral, and little did she know at that time that her own funeral would be a few weeks later.

Living through these traumatic death experiences brought thousands of flashbacks into my mind. There were the happy times as children, our loving family, our church, and supporting friends. There were the hard times of crop failure, loss of the dairy business, poverty, and sickness to remember. There were the times of spiritual uplifting, the days at church camp, the parties we had in our childhood home for our many friends; and then there were the days with boyfriends coming to visit, the dating stage, and our respective marriages followed by two daughters being divorced and remarried. There were the days when our parents relished every moment they could have with their grandchildren. There was the bonding of my grandfather with my two sons, which fulfilled his own dreams of having the sons which he never had. There was the week before my father died when he requested that I change my last name to Kellogg because he felt that he was not leaving a Kellogg legacy for his family. That seemed so important to him. What a host of flashbacks entered my mind during this period. It was as if all of life was being shown on a screen before my mind.

It had only been a few years in which I had finally healed emotionally from the many different scars which I had developed throughout much of my life. It became obvious to me at a very young age that my father wanted a boy and that I would be treated in many ways as if I were the boy for which he longed. I had to learn to be tough, strong, work hard, and essentially perform what was then seen as a man's job in life. My father told me later in life while I was single that I didn't need a man in my life, because I was able to do everything myself; however, I felt the need for a companion whom I could love and respect. Many times in first marriage, I felt all alone because of negative comments and lack of emotional support. The total responsibility of raising and supporting our children seemed to fall on my shoulders. How could my husband who was graciously ministering to the elderly, counseling young couples, preaching, and performing weddings be so negative or literally absent in our marriage? It was as if my commitment to God to marry him and make the best of it had turned sour without even the slightest hint of gratitude, respect, love, responsibility, support, or approval. The decision to divorce was one of giving a gift of freedom to him at his request while at the same time removing myself and my children from a totally negative situation. I believed it would be better to live alone and be there for my children than to continue in such an unpredictable marriage not knowing when he would flare up again. I knew that if anything happened to me, he would not able to care for our children since he was not caring for us while we were a family.

It was additionally painful when the people who were being ministered to by my husband during the divorce would come to me and ask how long it might take for me to reconcile with him. I never attempted to describe to them the problems in my marriage. No one would have believed that a person, who seemed so wonderful to them, could be so hurtful to me.

When I began dating Ken in August of 1992, I cried every time he was appreciative, caring, and respectful; gave gifts to me; or shared in my workload. He asked to marry me, and I was so afraid to marry again that I cried every time he said anything about it. I was embarrassed and humiliated at my frequent tears and tried to figure out why I was crying. It finally dawned on me that every time I cried, it was because his caring expressions, comments, or gifts were the exact opposite of situations in which I had been hurt so many times. It was hard for me to accept this new unconditional love for which I had longed all my life. Needless to say, it took two full years before I could accept his love without shedding tears. The idea of marriage still frightened me. It was hard to trust again. I knew in my heart that I could trust him and that I would never leave him, and because of that confidence, I finally agreed to marriage. Still, it took nearly another three to four years of tears and crying before I healed and felt truly happy again. The contrast in my life could never have been greater. I have never had to worry about an angry threat, not being appreciated or loved, or about his affections being showered on other people and especially women as had happened so many times during my first marriage.

CHAPTER 39

ART OF GIVING

"Give and it shall be given unto you" comes to mind every time I give a gift to someone else. Giving without expecting anything in return is truly a wonderful expression of love. We have been told in sermons that you can't out give God, and that is literally true. It's a little bit like the comparison with small tributaries which feed the Mississippi River. It just keeps on giving and rolling along as the song says. In a way, in my life money has seemed disconnected from the work required to earn it. I think that may only happen when a person is truly doing what they want to do in life and possibly even more so if it is for an eternal purpose. I well remember when I accepted my first teaching position. I wanted that job for the experience of teaching children and so I could be a positive influence in their lives. Of course, I knew that I would be receiving wages for this teaching contract, and that was important but not the highest priority in my mind. At any rate, I was thoroughly enjoying my new job, which was to create a new kindergarten program and teach the children to read very early. One day, the principal came into my classroom and handed me a check. I will never forget how surprised I was and the feeling that I had when receiving a payment or wages for doing what was so enjoyable and personally rewarding for me. I have always had that reaction to receiving wages. If you are doing what you enjoy, it will never feel like work.

It brings great pleasure to be able to give to others. The whole premise in our private-school business is that we are giving a superb education that will benefit these children for a lifetime. It would be nice if it could be given to them free. It is necessary, we believe, to provide an excellent private educational program that is in all ways superior to public education but for the least dollars possible. It is imperative to be able to pay respectable wages and benefits as well as to provide for growth in our business at the same time. We believe in presenting a solid, religious, nondenominational foundation for all children, including saying grace at mealtimes and prayers in their monthly Bible club.

It is a pleasure to give gifts to our employees and to provide extra opportunities for special drawings and other perks. Many of our employees have already received gifts for which they are always thankful and of which they speak so highly. We provide a matching retirement plan as well as bonuses for our employees. I do not want anyone to feel as if they are performing work that is not enjoyable for them. If employees are happy, they will be able to spread that happiness among their children. We have truly seen God's blessings upon our schools, our employees, our children, and their families.

Giving is an art similar to unconditional love. The giver cannot expect anything in return. Love and hate cannot live in the same heart at the same time, as is stated in the Bible that sweet and bitter water do not come from the same well.

CHAPTER 40

LESSONS FROM HISTORY

It is said that history is the best teacher. Everyone should study history because there is so much to learn. What happened between Cain and Abel? What happened with Joseph and his brothers? What happened with Noah, his friends, and family? Why did Sarah turn into a pillar of salt? On and on throughout biblical times as well as more recent history, there are lessons to learn; otherwise, people will constantly repeat the same mistakes over and over again.

Even in politics in our country, it seems as if the pendulum swings back and forth between the Democrats and the Republicans. Do we or our children really study history and understand the underlying philosophy in our democratic system? It is of great concern to me that our liberal media and many liberal leaders are trying to undermine religious freedom as well as the ability to be in private business, hire employees, and try to improve our world conditions. It is also of grave concern that we can never seem to reach a stage of peace in the world. If we truly understood Bible prophesy, we would more readily realize that these wars and troubles with wars were prophesied years ago. What we must learn is how to stay in tune with our Heavenly Father and let Him guide us through these troubled times.

Now that Dale has passed to his eternal life, I wonder if he might be able to review his life while he was on earth from a different perspective. I wonder if we might have been able to live our married life together happily as we promised and planned on the day of our wedding. I wonder if the history which has now been written into the lives of our children and grandchildren could have been happy, fulfilling, and healthy as opposed to being somewhat fragmented, often painful, and even embarrassing to our families and friends. I wonder what I could have done differently. I wonder if his last relationship with the young Asian nurse, "the mother of all love," as he excitedly told my husband and I, was really the reenactment of his first true love with the clockmaker's daughter he left in northern Korea. Interestingly, his love life went full circle. I wonder if he had married the clockmaker's daughter and brought her to the USA, might he have lived his life full of happiness. I wonder if the resentment and frustration which he portrayed to me and our children during our marriage was the "acting out" of his frustration at not being able to continue his original and deepest loving relationship with his first true lover? I also wonder how many other times the young Asian nurse befriended elderly men in order to become the recipient of bequeaths in their will, as she received from him. I wonder about the cultural trait of servitude which is taught to young girls in many cultures? Some cultures teach their children to serve others and always try to please their masters; whereas in our culture children seem to grow up playing and having fun. Once a man has experienced the feeling of being the master in a relationship and being treated with such adoration and servitude, he may never be able to adjust, accept and enjoy the equality and team effort that is required and which usually exists within a typical American marriage.

Certainly there were many unfortunate happenings in Dale's life which could have caused the underlying fate of our marriage. Our real life marriage should have been the greatest loving family that anyone could ever have. It was the tragedy of that unfulfilled lifetime family relationship for which I grieved at his passing. It had been my expectation that at some point during his lifetime, we would have been able to forgive, and rebuild our family. Nearly a week after his passing, I suddenly felt an assuring peace that Dale, in his heavenly home, was now able to understand and be at peace. The bond of my love for him had never changed over the years even though his actions required that I set him free.

CHAPTER 41

DISCIPLINE OF FOCUSING

One of the most difficult lessons to learn in life is how to focus our minds on the lessons being taught or on the task at hand. We have all known people we refer to as being scatterbrained. Learning to focus is rarely taught in school. Focusing cannot be acquired without a person being able to organize their thoughts and the tasks at hand. If there is not a focused direction in a person's daily life, it might be assumed that that person will merely drift or float through life with things always happening in life which will change his or her direction. It is like being tossed to and fro with every gust of the wind as stated in the Bible. It is also like building a house upon the sand and having your house crumble when the rains come.

Focusing is an exercise in which one learns to control thoughts and become productive in using the thought process. For example, if a child is learning to work a math problem but is thinking about lunch or recess or looking out the window and dreaming about going on vacation, he probably will never be able to complete a math problem, much less a whole assignment. Children with a problem in focusing rarely receive good grades or feel proud of their accomplishments in school. They often become daydreamers and rarely make it through school. They often drop out of school or graduate with a diploma that is for all practical purposes useless.

It is my opinion that contrary to what I was taught in college, the intelligence quotient or IQ as it is called can be changed by quantum leaps. Remembering the research which was performed on monkeys in which an equal number of monkeys were stroked daily and shown attention and love and another equal number of monkeys were ignored. The result of this experiment proved that love and attention were necessary for life, whereas the monkeys who were ignored died within a short period of weeks. I don't believe a similar formal research project has ever been done with human beings regarding their intelligence quotient; however, I strongly suspect that the results would shock every parent and teacher. We were taught in the early fifties that students should be grouped according to their intelligence and ethnic ability levels in reading and math and that each group could be expected to progress at an average speed. That was pretty much the status quo in the public schools in which I taught in Iowa, Minnesota, and later in California.

I broke through that limited expectation level soon after owning my first private school. I discovered that very young children could master levels of achievement far above what I had previously been taught and had been led to believe. Perhaps my first eye-opener came when our child-star student, Rodney Allen Rippey, would greet me as he entered school each day with a huge smile and a very intelligent and adultlike greeting. He was always well composed, articulate, considerate, and intelligent in his manner of speaking. He would be the first to say "Good morning, how are you today?" After I returned a greeting to him, he would add another comment of great interest for that particular day, such as "I am so very excited about our upcoming field trip tomorrow! Do you think the weather will be sunny?" I was amazed at his repertoire. Rodney was African American and an excellent student.

Everything I did and said to my own children from the minute they were born, I believed, would shape their lives, their interests, and their personalities. I felt that raising them was the most critical job of intense teaching that I could ever perform. Every single minute was important for stimulating their minds and involving them in cognitive, motor skill, and social development.

Court-appointed visitations after the divorce made it increasingly more urgent for me for quality and persistent teaching of my children. Suddenly they were receiving different experiences in their lives. They were now being allowed to attend one or more movies every other weekend, ample leisure time for watching television, and whatever happened would happen. I prayed that the influence I had with them would be stronger than the more lackadaisical lifestyle that they were now experiencing.

I believe that the time spent focusing and teaching my children to be focused and well organized rose to the top like cream rising in fresh milk. I believe that had they experienced that double life during their first five to seven years that they might not have survived as well. I am thankful for their brilliance, strength, wisdom, spiritual attunement, and their ability to understand not why but what happened in their lives and to deal with it in a mature manner.

CHAPTER 42

VIEWING THE PASSAGE OF TIME IN THE REARVIEW MIRROR

L ife would be so much simpler if we could review our life periodically and then see a rerun as if on a video and then have the opportunity to make changes we might consider necessary for a better life experience. Many of us have that opportunity in sports or in rehabilitation therapy. Just today, I spoke with a lady who had taken a ski lesson here at Breckenridge Ski Resort in Colorado. She was thrilled because for the first time she was able to observe herself skiing on a video and then go directly back to the ski slope and improve her skiing technique. Wouldn't it be wonderful if we could do the same thing in life? Wouldn't it be great of we could have at least one rerun in life, particularly in the case of an accident which we could not foresee but from which we might suffer for months or years?

I had such an experience that I would have liked to have had an opportunity to correct before it happened, but that is why it is called an accident because it was unintentional and unexpected. I had joined a ski club that had a ski trip planned to Mammoth, California, in February of 1982. I did not know anyone in the group, but it was a church group from the Crystal Cathedral in Garden Grove, California. I had seen the advertisement in the church bulletin and having gone skiing only with my own family prior to that, I thought this might be a weekend that would be fun and I might meet some interesting people.

I left my car in the church parking lot and boarded the bus. It seemed as if everyone else knew each other, and they definitely were in a partying mood. The only empty seat was next to a kind-looking gentleman, and we had interesting conversations mostly about politics since he was a city councilman for the city of Cypress, as I remember. Since I had been involved in politics in Sacramento in the field of education and had written and lobbied for several bills, we talked for several hours until the bus we were riding in broke down when we were nearly to Bishop. It took several hours for another bus to be sent to us from Orange County, which made our arrival in Mammoth at about two on a Saturday morning. Everyone was very tired, but we were to be ready to board the bus again at 7:00 a.m. for our ride to Mammoth Ski Resort. Everyone had a great day skiing, and as it began to snow heavily late that afternoon, we were again shuttled back to our lodge on the charter bus. From there we walked to town in the deep new snow. It was beautiful. It snowed heavily all night long, and there was almost zero visibility the next morning. I debated with myself as to whether I really should ski in such a heavy blizzard or instead to wait in my small room until the scheduled bus departure at 3:30 p.m. that day. I was still tired from lack of sleep and a hard day skiing on Saturday; but my final decision was to leave on the 7:00 a.m. bus, ride up on the earliest ski lift, and then plan to only ski midway to the lodge and stay there all day relaxing and socializing . . . something that I really had never done before. I was a little worried as I rode up on the seven thirty ski lift with the workers who were servicing the mountain. Barry, the person with whom I visited on the bus on the trip to Mammoth, happened to get on the same chair lift as I did. We commented about how heavily the snow was coming down and that it was nearly zero visibility. I remarked that I only intended to ski to the lodge, which is only about three hundred yards, and that I was going to sit the storm out. After getting off the ski lift, I had trouble seeing the snow below me. Barry and several others began skiing along what is known as the Wall. I found lack of visibility very disorienting; and the snow was very deep, heavy, and wet. As I made my second or third traverse, I seemed to lose my sense of equilibrium because it was a total "white out." I began a turn to the right; my skis came to a sudden stop, stuck into the deep, heavy snow when I heard a loud crack in my right femur and fell over with my head pointing down the fairly steep slope. I instantly knew the severity and the seriousness of my injury as my mind raced and I prayed for strength and endurance to get through this calamity. No one was with me at the time; however, several skiers whom I had never met or known before stopped and stayed vigil around me until the rescue workers arrived at their jobs. Additionally, Barry, who was with the group, heard about my accident, and he sidestepped back to where I would remain for well over an hour and a half. It was very cold, and I was being buried in the new falling snow, which different people brushed off from me from time to time. My mind was extremely active during that whole day. I plotted and planned for all the changes that would need to happen in my life because of the broken leg. Finally, the ski patrol rescued me; and I had a very nervous ride in his sled, headed down the steep mountainside to the first-aid room at chair one. It took until 12:30 p.m. until I arrived at the Mammoth Hospital. The surgeon on duty had just completed another surgery and said that my surgery would have to be scheduled for the next day. Nurses tried in vain to reach my Kaiser insurance carrier in order to receive approval to schedule a surgery. The answer they received was that I would have to be transported to Los Angeles for the surgery. I explained that I had $15,000 available in order to pay cash for the surgery, but they were not allowed to accept cash from someone who was insured with another company. So we waited while the doctor went to lunch and returned at one thirty, at which time he ordered everyone to prepare for my surgery. He had decided that it would be too dangerous to wait another day with the extent of my spiral femur fracture and the separation of the bones. I insisted on an epidural because I had allergic reactions to most anesthetics. The surgeon called for an assistant surgeon and two nurses, and then I was prepared for a five-and-a-half-hour surgery.

I was awake during the whole surgery. And never in my life had I imagined the hard work of surgery, not, that is, until I observed firsthand how hard the surgeons and nurses had to work in order to set my leg; drill into the hip bone and attach a Richards plate to the femur with a giant screw which screwed into the hip bone; and then four additional screws were screwed through the Richards plate into the femur. Part of the complications were due to the fact that the hospital did not have the right screws on hand and the blizzard was so severe that no one could drive to another hospital to get the right screws. Another complication was because an epidural only blocks pain but does not relax muscles, and since my muscles were very strong, it was like a tug-of-war for both doctors to try to pull the spiral break apart enough to set it properly. They made three attempts and felt that it was still not quite right, but I told them to leave it and I would make the best of it for the rest of my life. They did agree, and then it seemed that they had to hammer and pound the screws with great strength and force into my bone. The main surgeon was sweating profusely and uttering some swear words as he struggled to complete the surgery and finally stitch the fifteen-inch incision in my thigh together. I felt so sorry for him that I even apologized during the surgery. Of course, having a patient talking during surgery did not help him at all, so I tried to be quiet and just pray silently.

The group that I had been traveling with boarded their bus on schedule and brought my suitcase to the hospital, leaving it with the receptionist at the front desk. One lady, Natalie, was very concerned about everyone leaving me there, knowing that I did not know anyone in that whole town.

The snowstorm continued for days upon days. It was one of the worst snowstorms in the history of that area. Within days, the snow was deeper than the hospital, and the window in my hospital room turned black because no light could get through more than twenty-five feet of snow. Dealing with this major surgery and swelling of my leg and the icing of it for twenty-four hours was really hard. Then I had my first bout with an elevated blood pressure and several blood transfusions. I finally turned on the TV in my room and heard that there was a new scare with blood transfusions whereby they were discovering AIDS in the nation's blood supply. The next day I was to meet my newly assigned therapist, who said that I had to stand up on my feet. I felt totally unable to sit up, much less get up. He patiently helped me up, taught me how to use a wheelchair, then a walker, and finally crutches. I was given lessons in which I had to learn to go up and down stairs. I never knew that walking could be so difficult. I was fifty years old at the time.

Eventually, a close friend of mine flew his private plane to pick me up. I was happy to be released from the hospital after thirteen days of rehabilitation, tending to my dozens of floral arrangements, managing my employees by telephone, and looking out the window at the deep snowdrifts after someone shoveled enough snow away from my window so that light could come in and I could see out again. My only visitors during that period were my children Cathy and David, who drove through the snowstorms to visit me and make sure that I was recuperating successfully. I was so very happy to see them.

The following year was difficult in that I continued working while walking on crutches, swimming many hours daily for non-weight-bearing exercise, but constantly enduring the most pain I had ever known. Finally, as the pain continued to increase and several doctors could not come up with any rationale for the pain, I made an appointment with a doctor at Childrens Hospital in Los Angeles, Dr. Sariemento Agusto, a visiting doctor from Greece. He took a long look at me and then simply said, "I don't understand why you have such severe pain, but I have enough time between surgeries tomorrow to remove the hardware in your leg." I agreed and again requested an epidural to deaden the pain. During the surgery as Dr. Agusto began removing the screws, I heard him exclaim, "Just look at these rusty screws. No wonder she was having so much pain!" I immediately remembered that during my surgery the year prior, the doctors did not have the proper hardware and could not get it due to the blizzard, so having incompatible metals in my body had caused an electrolytic type reaction, and the metals were corroding and causing pain. As the doctor was throwing the hardware into the trash, I asked him so save the hardware for me, which I still have today. During that surgery, a friend of the anesthesiologist came to the door to visit with him; but while he was in the hallway, I noticed that my blood pressure began dropping to about 50/30. I knew this was dangerous, so I told the surgeon, who sternly called the anesthesiologist back into the room to correct and monitor my blood pressure. I believe that if I had been under general anesthetic, I might not have made it through that surgery without complications. After the surgery, I was wheeled to the recovery room, where several other patients were recovering but were entirely covered with sheets. The nurses were talking and referred to dirty patients, so I immediately called a nurse over and asked what *dirty patients* meant. She said that I was not supposed to be awake, but that those patients had

AIDS. I asked to be moved to my private room immediately, and she called my doctor and received authorization.

My recovery was rather rapid after the removal of the hardware, but a second year on crutches was required, after which I absolutely could not seem to regain the ability to walk correctly. It took several therapy sessions and much concentrated study of everyone else's walk in order to finally get the feel and the rhythm back. My next obsession was to ski again, so three years after my accident, I was back on skis; but needless to say, my subconscious mind froze with fear. It was a major breakthrough when, after much coaxing from my friends, I was able to turn my skis and traverse back and forth down the mountainside. Now, after more than twenty years, I am still enjoying my favorite outdoor sport, which forever will remind me of our passage through life taking this trail or that one; making this choice or that one; and trying to avoid accidents along the way. The beauty of the crystal-white snow against the tall dark green pine trees with tiny villages and/or mountain tops in the distance is tranquil as compared to the busy, heavily populated, and traffic-laden cities in which we live. It is very much like viewing the passage of time through the rearview mirror.

CHAPTER 43

CHILDREN, GRANDCHILDREN, NIECES, AND NEPHEWS

G randchildren have a special place in the hearts of grandparents especially when they are as endearing as mine have been. Now I can understand why my mother always said that she enjoyed working in schools because children were so delightful. I think my mother retained her childlike love for life even in her final year living in her paralyzed condition. She was always happy, had a good sense of humor, and laughed a lot. It would have been much more difficult to have cared for her so intensely if she had been sad, depressed, cranky, or worried about things. This may also be a hidden rule of longevity, to be happy with a good sense of humor, and be able to laugh a lot. Don't they say that laughter is the best medicine? Maybe it is really true.

Grandchildren have a kinship which no other children can have with you. They are genetically related, and traits of great-grandparents or even great-great grandparents sometimes appear out of nowhere. These children are, in fact, born of our flesh one generation after another. Is it any wonder that we as grandparents might have great expectations as well as admiration for these miracle children? I can understand how the pendulum swings in that children who were raised in a strict discipline environment might react and as parents, like Dr. Spock, think that their children should have the freedom to be whatever and act however they choose. Without this explanation, we could never understand the hippies of the sixties or the druggies of the seventies and eighties. Where has the rationale gone regarding the reasons why successful children didn't grow to become responsible adults without the guidance and watchful prayerfulness of their parents? If parent accountability is thrown out the window, could it be any surprise that we are seeing so many rebellious teenagers who are committing crime and suicide at such increasing rates? We are also seeing an increasing number of unmarried young mothers who are not ready for the commitment and responsibility which are required to raise a child. They are the ones who often leave their child or children for grandparents to care for and essentially raise.

There is a delicate veil between the grandparent and the grandchild by which the younger generations feel that they are independent, somewhat removed from the grandparent, and can act and behave however they choose. Any admonishment from a grandparent is sometimes interpreted as "being mean" or "not approving of the child" or "not accepting" of that child who now has developed his or her own self-righteous, self-designed style of resentment or resistance. My advice and personal reaction to this phenomenon whereby the grandchild has deliberately broken off a relationship is to relinquish any further expectation of that child and simply wait and see if the child will ever seek out a bonding or a friendship with the grandparent in the future. One cannot push against resistance. Only a caring, supportive, prayerful attitude will provide the positive position for mutual respect and communication.

Nieces and nephews do not carry the same feeling of familial responsibility. They can enjoy their anonymity and relationship as being one step farther removed from the immediate family. This distance usually provides more room for acceptance and appreciation for their own uniqueness than if they are being considered a direct descendent with all the hopes and expectations that such a relationship entails.

CHAPTER 44

DEVALUATION OF THINGS

Very young children treasure things, toys, coins, and eventually dollars. It is not until after much hard work in life and when a person has reached a plateau on which he or she feels that the basic needs in life are comfortably met that a person can begin to look more realistically at other priorities. Some of these priorities might include marriage, having a baby, purchasing a home, traveling, building a business, or even volunteering services wherever one sees a need. There does come a time when things that were held to be of great importance or value seem to lose their appeal. Particularly when one is faced with a terminal illness, for example, all priorities seem to suddenly shift. The value of time spent with a loved one or with children becomes more important, eating habits may change as one seeks a healthier diet, and spiritual things become more important and rise to the forefront. When a person loses the ability to walk, that skill then becomes the most important focus of his life. If one can no longer talk, eat, or sleep, whatever the deprivation that one took for granted now becomes the central drive in one's life to correct or learn to adapt to a different focus in life. Other things in life realign themselves as to being devalued in comparison. Age is another factor where great value was placed on strength, agility, perhaps even beauty and grace while a person is young. It seemed then as if one could be young forever, and time seemed to pass very slowly. During middle age, there is still a very strong feeling of well-being and a denial that one would ever enter old age like the elderly people we see everywhere are. There is a wide gap between middle age and being "over the hill," a common reference to people over fifty.

My own personal philosophy has always been to look at where I am in life or at what I have acquired and then think of myself in the position of being twenty or thirty years older, for example, and then thinking how much I would desire to be the very age that I am at the present. That always makes me feel young and appreciate my current youthfulness as compared to how it might be thirty years down the road. That also works for me in the area of acquisitions. I may be striving for expansion in my business or property holdings, but even if I only had as much as I did when I was living in poverty, I feel thankful to be at this place in my life knowing that my value in life is not in how much I have acquired but in the relevancy of using my acquisitions to further my service to mankind. The same principles work in the area of health. I may wish that I were 100 percent healthy, but if I look around at family; friends, and people in the news, I am truly thankful to be as healthy as I am. Additionally, one gains a greater sense of empathy when the focus is on helping and giving to others. I understand that research also shows that the person who is helping others will ultimately live a much longer, happier, and healthier life. So let's go for it!

CHAPTER 45

SIFTING THROUGH LIFE FOR VALUATION

Many times, children in school and people in general cannot sift through all the episodes and events that come their way each and every day and still be able to prioritize their energy, time, and goals. Some people think it is easier to drift along in life, get up late, and put everything off until it is convenient or even until tomorrow, letting television, phone calls, children, or friends dictate whatever happens during that day. We all know people who say "whatever happens will happen." Essentially, this might be a little like trying to drive a car in neutral. Minutes, hours, days, weeks, months, and even a lifetime might be lost in this mode or frame of mind.

It takes a lot of discipline and effort in order to prioritize your time and energy. Without spending the time and energy up front in order to organize and prioritize your affairs for each day, it would be similar to starting out on a long trip or journey and meandering down the highways of our country without a map. Another example might be to leave the marked ski trail and ski out of bounds, thinking that an avalanche could never happen to me. There are constraints in life which assist in keeping us safe on the highways, the bicycle paths, swimming in the ocean riptides, or in almost every place where there might be danger. Unbeknownst to children growing up, there may be severe dangers in certain television programs, in nearby gangs, in illegal drugs; and there is even the possibility of kidnappers lurking in the neighborhood or in the shopping malls.

Unless children are taught at a very early age to know the value of what they see, hear, say, taste, feel, and do, they may never be able to cultivate a value system. Teaching skills to children in junior high school is much more difficult than in the primary grades. Teaching children at age five who already have a good foundation which was instilled in them by their parents from infancy to age five is the easiest teaching of all. It is imperative that we in our country begin to understand that the first five years are the most important years in brain development. There is also considerable research now that indicates that a great amount of learning already is beginning in the womb.

The recent birth of a baby, who weighed only eight ounces and went home from the hospital perfectly healthy at five pounds, should dispel the notion of the proabortionists who advocate that the growth in the mother's womb is not a baby until after it is born. With the shortage of men in our country due to our many wars, I would think that the millions of babies aborted by now would dwarf the number of persons who have been killed in all wars. I don't know if those statistics are available, but I'm sure someone will research those figures. Our value system regarding human life does not make sense. One step further in this argument is the fact that a mother can be sentenced to life for murder for killing her newborn baby or even leaving it to die minutes after giving birth; however, a doctor can assist the mother in killing the baby prior to birth by crushing the baby's skull with a sharp instrument and it will be perfectly legal. The other argument which I would have against the mother's right to choose is to question when in the lineup of our human value system is the parents' right to choose more important than that of their unborn baby. I might not have been here had my own mother listened to friends and relatives who chided "Have an abortion since we are in a depression!" Having made difficult choices most of my life, for me it is inconceivable to realize that at one time in my life when I was not yet capable of making a choice, I could have been aborted, but I believe my mother made the right choice. I am thankful for her decision.

Beyond the values of human life, there are thousands of choices which need to be made every single day by every living person. Having the ability to sort through myriads of choices is an indispensable skill which needs to be mastered at a very young age.

CHAPTER 46

REFLECTING ON NARROW ESCAPES

If a cat is said to have nine lives, then I must already have lived more lives than that. Reflecting back on my life, I am convinced that there has been divine intervention at least nine times. First there was the decision to save my life from abortion. Then there were the severe cases of rheumatic fever in my childhood in which many other children with the same disease either suffered mental retardation or died. Our neighbor's daughter suffered an even milder case of rheumatic fever the same year that I was ill in 1941 and she was committed to a mental institution for the remainder of her thirty years of life. Additionally there was my episode which was diagnosed as polio when I was fifteen from which I might never have recovered. Certainly I was beginning to feel that the hand of God was interceding on my behalf and that He had something important for me to do in my life which was being spared.

Later in life and during my travels throughout the world, I met with other life threatening dangers which I will mention here briefly. There was a scuba diving trip which had been planned to the Great Barrier Reef in Australia. There was a three-day stopover at the beginning of the trip to the Fiji Islands, and reservations were made for the Hilton Hotel on the beachfront. I noticed when our plane was landing on Fiji Island that it was raining heavily; however, I did not think too much about a tropical rainstorm until we arrived at the hotel. A large sign was posted in the lobby, stating that the lounge and restaurant would be closed due to the typhoon which was rapidly approaching. Quickly I said to our traveling group that I believed we should cancel our reservations, return immediately to the airport, and take the next flight to Australia. Unfortunately, the flight which we had been on had left already, and all flights incoming and outgoing had been cancelled until further notice. Crowds were forming in the airport with the same idea of leaving Fiji as soon as possible if not sooner.

My reaction was to suddenly became very persistent, and I begged the airline agents to relocate our group to the safest location on the island. Finally, after making many phone calls on my behalf the agent told me that there was one room, which could accommodate four persons, available at a very, very old motel on a hill about a mile and a half away from the airport. We were immediately on our way with the last taxi available speeding us to that motel. People were literally running for shelter, and workers were pounding boards over windows and doors as we drove past houses and shops. By this time, it was late in the evening, and I certainly did not feel like eating dinner. I looked for the safest place to hide in case the storm worsened. I reasoned that the most protected place would be in the shower, which seemed to have very thick walls and where no broken glass could reach me. I placed pillows and blankets in the shower and proceeded to get as comfortable as possible. Everyone else went to dinner, and the motel was nearly empty except for me in my makeshift fortress in the shower.

At approximately 7:30 p.m., the noise from the storm sounded like the whole earth was shaking, and then I heard someone trying to force open each motel-room door. A couple of men ran down the hallway from door to door screaming, "Evacuate immediately, evacuate immediately, come quickly, everyone must get out immediately!" Now I really began to feel fear as it was dark, and those of us who were rounded up were being forced to follow the men outside into the storm and then into the nearby restaurant. Walking about fifty feet along a sidewalk took strength and perseverance, more than we ever thought that we could muster. The wind was so strong that it was forcing twigs and leaves into the concrete walls of the motel. Roofs from other buildings were flying overhead and noisily crashing onto the ground nearby. Coconuts were bouncing everywhere. Then we were told to immediately crowd together underneath a heavy large circular wooden bar counter tabletop. There were approximately twenty-five of us, all natives except for our small group, which now huddled together as if bound together by saran wrap. It was skintight under there. The native men on the periphery of our compact group faced out and held chairs in front of their faces with the legs pointing toward the entrance doors. Amazingly, we were being pelted by salty ocean spray which was pounding this motel and restaurant a mile and a half from the ocean. Our faces were covered with saltwater, and our clothing was drenched. We expected the big eight-foot-high decorative wooden entrance doors to be crashing into us at any moment. We sat, praying silently, facing possible death but all the while praying to be spared while the typhoon raged and roared for over two and a half hours. Suddenly it became silent—deafeningly silent. I whispered to the persons who were pressed tightly against me and asked if we were all right. Someone whispered to be quiet because now we were in the eye of the storm. Sure enough, within minutes, the roaring, crashing, and spewing of ocean water began again and continued relentlessly until 1:30 a.m. when again it stopped suddenly with deadening silence. At that exact moment, the natives stood silently and walked single file out of the restaurant some with children in their arms as if they were leaving a movie theater after an impressive show which had a sad ending.

The next morning and for the next several days, we lived among the natives who were dealing with the aftermath of death and destruction. The radar unit in the airport had been knocked out, and there would be no flights in or out for at least ten days. There was no drinking water available, and the one little grocery store nearby was stripped of all food. People wandered around sorting through the remains of their meager possessions if they could find them. The little old motel where we had stayed weathered the storm very well. It obviously had weathered many such storms over the years.

We learned that thirty people were killed in that storm. The people who had run and sought shelter in the public school nearby were all killed when the concrete walls fell and crushed them from the force of winds reaching 110 miles an hour. Many people in the Hilton Hotel, where we originally had our reservations, were drowned as the waves crashed through their oceanfront sliding-glass doors. They had become trapped within their rooms and washed out to sea as the waves crashed in and forced them against their entrance doors. The doors in the rooms opened in rather than out toward the hallway. Cattle and horses were lying dead everywhere, and coconuts were severely scarred as they had bounced throughout the countryside, against walls and vehicles during the storm. There was devastation everywhere.

Our next priority was to try to leave Fiji. We returned to the airport to find that no planes could land for a week to ten days, except for one emergency Air New Zealand plane which was equipped with its own radar system and would be landing within minutes. I discovered that our little group could board that plane if we had cash for the airfare. It would be landing and leaving within only ten minutes. That was the fastest that I ever had to move, but we boarded that emergency flight not even knowing where we were going. At that point, I did not care where the plane was going, but I knew that we had to leave immediately. So in shorts and T-shirts, we boarded the plane which was bound for Tokyo, Japan. Landing in Tokyo, we found it to be snowing and very cold. Fortunately I had a sweat outfit in my carry on luggage which I put on over my other clothing immediately after exiting the plane. I called home to tell my mother that I was okay, but she was surprised and had no knowledge that I had even been in a storm. We bought the next available tickets to California and were never more thankful to be home and alive. I never did get to the Great Barrier Reef.

Then there was my trip to China with a river cruise on the Yangtze River. It was a wonderful trip; and I was thrilled to observe the Chinese people working the countryside, growing vegetables, fishing, and doing their laundry as we sailed past. I had elected to take a side trip up a fjord on a small enclosed motorboat which held about twelve persons. After departing from the cove where the cruise ship was anchored, I detected that there were no life jackets on our small boat. We were pushing upstream in heavy turbulent waters when suddenly our boat lurched and grounded on rocks. Knowing already that there were no life jackets, I became extremely alarmed noting that the currents were much too swift to swim to shore and that the driver of our boat not only did not speak English but also seemed to think that by racing the engine he could dislodge our boat from the rocks. Fumes from the engine racing were drifting into the boat, causing us to become sick, but no one had any solution to our problem. Finally, after about an hour in this situation, another boat came along, tied up to our boat, and maneuvered our boat back and forth until finally it dislodged. We were on our way again with all twelve passengers clapping their hands robustly.

Later in that trip, we toured the Tiananmen Square in Beijing; however, our tour guide cautioned us, severely stating that there was unrest and that we should not walk very far away from our tour bus. It would be important to video this scene, and so I proceeded alone toward the procession of people who were waiting in line to view statutes and a funeral memorial. There were thousands of Chinese people demonstrating, chanting, and it looked and felt dangerous. I began to have a strange sensation while I was videoing and trying to scan a 360-degree swath. It became apparent as I turned around that there was also a group of about six young Chinese men behind me turning exactly as I did. They were watching every move I made and obviously were spying on me. Quickly I sensed danger; noticing that my heart was racing and that I was becoming very tense, I moved back toward the bus as quickly as I could. We left within a few minutes and soon learned that was the beginning of the famous revolt and standoff in Tiananmen Square. Hundreds were killed, and our tour bus was the last bus to be able to leave that area safely. Once again, I felt that God was watching over and protecting me.

The following year in 1981, I joined a tour group of eighteen people for a three-week guided bus tour throughout Soviet Russia and the Baltic countries. Our tour group was in Lithuania when the Lithuanians were using tractors to topple statues of Stalin from their bridges and in their parks. They were denouncing communism and claiming their independence from the Soviet Union. While we were there and just after breakfast, the Soviet tanks started drivling into town in order to take over Lithuania again. Our tour guide, who had lived her whole life under Communist rule, began crying and told us that she was not sure what kind of a tour we might have that day. She said it looked as if war was ready to begin any minute. Nonetheless, we began our tour and took several detours in order to avoid the military confrontation. As we drove past a small park, I noticed that children were walking to school, oblivious of the situation. When they spotted a Soviet army tank parked at the corner of the park, even though there were Soviet soldiers in it, the children gleefully climbed up on top of it. The soldiers seemed to ignore the children, knowing that they had bigger fights to fight that day. We learned about many families who had teenage boys whom the soldiers dragged out of their homes and instantly used them in the Soviet army. They had no forewarning whatsoever of their impending fate. A little taste of communism that day made me more appreciative than ever before of our freedom in America.

There was also a joyride which I took with my pilot friend. We had left early in the morning on a Fourth of July, flying out of Anchorage, Alaska. We were going to attend a Salmon Bake celebration which was being held at a gold-mining town. My camera was loaded with film, and I was expecting to take pictures. While we were flying, I noticed a very old gold mine which looked very intriguing and I requested that we circle around the area so that I could get better pictures. As I was clicking the shutter, I heard the pilot make an outburst and instantly enter a steep climb. Unbeknown to either of us, there was a large steel cable which was drawn from high on the mountain across to the other side of the gold mine, and the bottom of our pontoons scraped the cable as the plane sought altitude. Not only was that a narrow escape from sure death, but it was also a reminder that life is short and an accident can instantly take your life away. We gave prayers of thanksgiving to God for His watchful care over us even when we were not aware that there was any imminent danger.

Narrow escapes, you might ask, or are they fortunate or coincidental? I believe that everything that happens in our lives is for a purpose, and possibly my purpose in life now is to tell my story for the sake of causing you as a reader to become more appreciative of life and the many ways in which our Heavenly Father intervenes in our lives. It is my prayer that you will accept the gift of salvation; live a full life; and enjoy a spiritual relationship with God and His Son, Jesus Christ, as a constant living presence in your life.

CHAPTER 47

ADVICE FOR GENERATIONS TO COME —
AN ETHICAL WILL

P robably the most difficult thing to do in life is to try to influence a younger generation especially children or grandchildren. Young people always think they know it all, but there was an old saying that I heard when I was young that said, "The older you get, the more you know. And the more you know, the more you realize the less you know." I didn't think that was possible; however, it is exactly true.

Spirituality, knowing and understanding the Bible and biblical truths, is the one solid truth upon which to build a life. Without this magnetic guidance from a Heavenly Father, life could not possibly have very much meaning, stability, or credibility. Younger children need to learn how the world and the universe were created by God. They will be stronger in withstanding the ridicule and criticism which they may receive from an atheistic, politically argumentative society and a liberal educational environment. Parents who state that they will let their children decide what to believe when they become old enough are doing a great disservice to those children. It would be better to have believed in God when a young child and to disavow that belief, if it must be, later in life than to never have believed at all.

It is important to distinguish between the Old Testament and the New Testament in the Bible. The Old Testament was written as a prophesy in which the shedding of the blood of a lamb would pay the price for cleansing of sins whereas the New Testament was written after Jesus, God's only son, shed his blood as the sacrifice for the sins of everyone who would believe in him and accept his salvation. The only prerequisite for receiving this sacrificial gift is to believe that Jesus was sent to be our Savior, admit to being of worldly or sinful nature without God, and turn and follow the paths that Jesus set forth in the New Testament.

Family values rate high on the list of priorities for living in this world of turmoil. Every child must have a solid foundation. I would rather believe in God and find out that there wasn't a God than to believe that there was *no* God and then find out later that there really was a God just as it states in the Bible. It is for this very reason that we provide a Bible club once a month for every child who attends our schools. A child may be excused with a written authorization letter in his or her cumulative record folder; however, usually those children who have been excused feel left out and usually either find a way to eavesdrop or else retaliate against the students who do attend the monthly half-hour Bible club. I have advised parents to allow their children to attend the nondenominational Bible clubs and then address their own religious differences at home so the child will have the opportunity to hear both religious viewpoints.

Personal philosophy is also important for each and every child to understand and develop. Children must begin to know what they believe and why as opposed to merely following in the shadow of the beliefs of their parents, their peers, or their mentors. A belief in God, the ability to communicate with others, and the ability to become self-reliant and self-sufficient are attributes which parents need to strive to instill into their young children.

Teaching children to take responsibility for their actions as well as the care of their personal items and that of the shared family home is the starting point. The circle of responsibility widens as a child matures. Any parent who attempts to wait until a child is five or possibly even ten until teaching them to share in the responsibilities of caring for the home will be shocked to learn that they have waited too long. The job of teaching a child responsibility begins as early as toilet training. Many times the responsibility of toilet training is also delayed by parents who are either lazy or indifferent to their duties. Obviously, a young child cannot take the lead and say, "Would you please begin teaching me how to care for myself?" I've always thought that parents should be required to pass a test in order to be allowed to give birth to a baby. How can it be that it requires a four-year degree plus another year of teacher training in order to be able to teach five-year-olds in kindergarten, but a parent can raise any number of children without a single course of instruction? It requires a license and coursework in order to get a job training dogs, but nothing is required to teach your own child. Does this make sense?

CHAPTER 48

BOTTOM LINE

Raising a child is the most important job in the whole world. Failure to train a child in a manner in which that child knows how to show respect, be honest, friendly, and kind to others requires a full-time educated and dedicated effort. Many children are saved almost as if by the seat of their pants by attending a well-qualified preschool. At least in an exemplary preschool, teachers have been trained in coursework which taught them how to motivate, instill a sense of responsibility, and build a solid educational foundation which will ultimately propel that child into a successful life. It is true that Abraham Lincoln was highly motivated and self-taught. Can we in today's lackadaisical environment find a highly motivated and self-taught person?

Parents who are not knowledgeable about child rearing should immediately begin taking courses or else hire a qualified trainer of children from the time the child is born; otherwise, I do not feel those persons should be in the business of raising children. Once again, I believe that parents who lack education in parenting skills should *not* be raising children. Children do not just grow like Topsy. Is it any wonder that we have discipline problems in schools, rebellious teenagers, graffiti artists, gang members, crime, murder, and rape running rampant in our country? When will we identify and do something to correct the bottom-line underlying problem?

Just think for a moment; if city planning commissioners were to begin allowing houses and commercial buildings to be built without architectural plans, certification, or approval, what chaos might happen with the first earthquake? If houses were no longer required to have a foundation or the soil compacted underneath, what stability would that house have in a heavy rainstorm or a hurricane? If that were to happen, we would begin to see the same collapse of our buildings as we are seeing in our younger generation of children.

If our country continues in the direction in which it is currently going, we may be heading in the direction of complete annihilation. If God or the church continues to be removed from our schools and our country, if abortions continue at the same rate of growth, if wars continue without ever ending, we might become the lost country of the twentieth century.

I remember visiting in Russia shortly after the collapse of the Soviet system of communism in the late 1980's. It had been decades since the churches had been closed and people were killed or tortured if they had a Bible, religious literature or were caught having an underground religious meeting during those years. We learned while touring Russia that the Communist leaders realized that the Russian people had become dispassionate, and crime was at the highest level ever in their history. It was during that period when no reference to God or religion was allowed that the moral deterioration of Russia became apparent. Finally the leaders allowed churches to be reopened and people were encouraged to return to their newly opened churches. After so many years of absence of any religious influence, the people whom I met simply did not know which church to attend. They did not have any religious leanings whatsoever. Interestingly enough, the church buildings with their stained-glass windows had been preserved. The church buildings themselves had been converted into different types of social meeting places such as opera halls, theaters, and movie houses.

It was important to me to be able to take a variety of small gifts to be given to Russian people whom I met on the street. The gifts included small American flags, packages of powdered milk, candy bars, inexpensive necklaces and about thirty small New Testament Bibles which I had printed in Russian ahead of time. My package of gifts were opened at the airport in Russia and were in the process of being confiscated when a Russian guard came over and demanded to know why I was bringing in so many Bibles. He said that only two Bibles would be allowed for one person. At that very moment the twenty people in our traveling group stated that they would each carry two of the Bibles and therefore the package was allowed. Later during the trip I offered the choice of a gift to friendly people whom I met on the streets. It was of great interest to me that the first choice was always for the Bible. Only one time did a young man choose the powdered milk because he said that he needed it for his baby. One elderly gentleman told me that he had wanted a Bible all of his life and this was the first one he had ever seen. He was so thankful that he held the Bible close to his heart and then gave me a small original oil painting which he had been hoping to sell. The second choice that people usually made was the American flag. They seemed to respect and show pride in holding the flag as they walked away. America, I believe is gradually lowering its standards similar to live lobsters being slowly brought to a boil for dinner. Americans seem unaware of their fate as politicians in our country gradually deprive our public school children of God, prayer, reverence, respect, patriotism, and the belief that freedom of speech only applies to those who seem to assist in the downward spiral of our nation. It is my hope and prayer that in America we will wake up before it is too late.

At the very least, churches and private schools are beginning to take up the slack and teach moral ethics, honor, and respect for God, family and our country before it is everlastingly too late. And that's the bottom line.

Attending a recent sixty year high school class reunion I discovered that our mutual core of small town love of family, God and country was never lost and is still central to our belief systems. Not one person out of two hundred and seventy-six graduates chose a path of disrespect of God, country or family or became involved in crime. One out of three completed their journey in this life early. Those of us who remain feel a deeper bond. Cliques which were evident in high school have disappeared, days of college, careers and raising a family are over and now everyone is focusing on the next lap in our mutual journey through the golden years of our lives.

Hiking up a mountain one day in southern California made me think how similar the hike was to our journey in life. There are different paths and the path which we choose is often exciting, sometimes difficult with detours and difficult climbs, but always an adventure toward a goal or a series of goals with new and changing vistas until reaching the peak or the mountain top.

Goal setting in life continues to be equally as important as it was when we first learned to walk, talk, read or become a contributing person in our society. The day when a person has no goals that person will begin shutting down. I have noticed a few people who set retirement as their ultimate goal and forgot to set further challenging goals. They often did not live very long. When asked when I am going to retire I usually comment that I will think about that when I reach 110 as I am constantly setting even more challenging goals to reach every single day.

Glimpses of several focus areas in my life in which I have been intensely involved have provided a kaleidoscope of experiences formulating the basis for my philosophy of life as well as the ideas and material for this book.

Underlying arenas which I have enjoyed include family, teaching, church leadership, banking, ranching, construction, business, talk show host and being a political advocate. Each arena included community appropriate to that particular path in this life. Each community was in fact separate and exclusive making the pathways seem as if they truly were nine separate lives to be lived and enjoyed to the fullest by one individual person and I am happy to have been so destined and to have the privilege to share my experiences, spiritual inclinations and partialities with you.

The basic thread throughout my life has been my core belief in God and His immeasurable love which allowed Him to send His only Son Jesus Christ, to earth to live amongst men and ultimately make amends for our worldly or sinful human nature and provide the way to set us straight again. By the way, the word sin originally meant missing the mark when shooting an arrow. Now, however, it means anything that would separate us from God's love, such as placing selfish interests and priorities ahead of God or simply not believing or acting like there is no God. After all, God did create man so that He could have fellowship with him. He in turn gave man the freedom of choice and many people choose to use that freedom to proclaim their disbelief in God their creator. This solid rock foundation has provided the strength, wisdom, and courage for me to make but a very small difference in this world. It would be my hope and prayer that you might also share in the knowledge of the love of God, His son Jesus Christ and the ever abiding presence of the Holy Spirit, that together one by one we can light the darkness of this world.

INDEX